Cooking with the Remoska

the official Remoska recipe cookbook

More than 200 recipes for use with the
Remoska multipurpose mini oven

recipes by
Milena Grenfell-Baines
Karina Havlů

published by
Hooray for Home Cooking Limited

Preston   England   2003

second edition

First published in 2003
Reprinted 2003

Hooray for Home Cooking Limited
PO Box 456
Preston Central
Preston
Lancashire
PR1 8GG

British Library Cataloguing in Publication Data
A catalogue record for this book is available from the British Library

ISBN No 0-9544900-0-2

Designed by
Gradwell Corporate Design
56 West Cliff
Preston PR1 8HU
England

Printed by
MIGER – reklamni agentura
1. máje 2609
756 64 Roznov p.R
Czech Republic

Contents

Acknowledgements

"I think you should write an English cookery book for the Remoska" said Ivo Svoboda, the marketing manager for the Remoska Company, I will introduce you to Karina Havlů....

Well, here it is, with my first thanks to Karina for allowing me to translate part of her Czech recipe book.

My very grateful thanks to my business partner Caterer, Derek Smith who cooked all the recipes for the photographs and tested many others.

To our company secretary and main 'taster' Jill Wadeson and my friend Joan Whittle – Catering Consultant with whom I worked for eight years broadcasting and demonstrating recipes, for reading and correcting the proofs (not to mention my grammar).

To Geoff Gradwell, creative director without whom this book would never have happened and to Jane Willis for the illustrations.

The photographs were taken by Ian Smith and Chris Hives of Metro Productions.

Thanks to my husband, George, family and friends who now take it for granted that the food they are served is almost always cooked in our Remoska!

Milena Grenfell-Baines

May 2003

Milena Grenfell-Baines

My interest in food began in 1950 when I went to France to be a governess in a family who employed a cook. Acquiring a taste for French food was no hardship and learning much from the family cook was a start. A few of the recipes in this book relate to those days.

For three years I worked from time to time in France as interpreter for cookery holidays, establishing two new cookery schools. I also occasionally worked with another agency promoting specialist cookery weekends across the UK and organised and demonstrated a number of cookery events both in Harrogate and Ambleside, in the Lake District.

With my good friend Joan Whittle, we organised, in my home town of Preston, for three successive years French, Austrian and Mediterranean cookery weeks which were featured on Granada TV. Granada also flew a team out to Nimes, Preston's twin town to follow a small group of my culinary colleagues and me, taking over a French restaurant for a week and serving a selection of British recipes to very appreciative French customers. In the early nineteen eighties, Joan and I broadcasted a weekly cookery programme on the newly established Red Rose Radio.

During those years I organised a very big food exhibition in the Preston Guild Hall called 'Hooray for Home Cooking'. Opened by Derek Cooper of the BBC Food Programme, it featured cookery demonstrations by such well known chefs as Paul Heathcote, Valentina Harris, Nigel Howarth and others and was the forerunner of the BBC Good Food Show now based in Birmingham.

Finding and introducing the Remoska to the British public has resulted in the fact that at an age when most people are well and truly retired, a colleague, one time head of catering college, now owner of a catering company, Derek Smith, and I have established our own company 'Hooray for Home Cooking' promoting the Remoska on our website and of course writing this book.

I have introduced Czech hotel and catering colleges to partners in the UK enabling Czech students to come for work and study experience.

I recently translated a CD Rom 'Modern Czech Cookery' available from our web site – **www.hoorayforhomecooking.com**

My other main interest is classical music and for the past 30 years I have had close involvement with the Royal Liverpool Philharmonic Orchestra and I am Chairman of Friends of the Orchestra. This has included cooking for conductors and soloists staying at our home and planning and taking Friends of the Phil on tours to the Czech Republic.

Coming to the UK as a refugee from the Nazis in 1939, most of my war years were spent in the Czechoslovak State Secondary School in Exile situated in Wales. At the end of World War 2, I decided to stay in England but remaining loyal to my Czech heritage, I was honoured in the year 2000 with the Jan Masaryk 'Gratis Agit' award, given by the Czech Minister of Foreign Affairs for remaining a faithful patriot and an ambassador of goodwill, culture and history of the Czech Republic.

In 1954 I married the architect Professor Sir George Grenfell-Baines, founder of the international firm Building Design Partnership. Soon I was entertaining clients to lunches and dinner parties, and with four children, cooking loomed large in the Grenfell-Baines household.

With two daughters, one living in France and one in Canada, grandchildren are scattered around the world. Some time ago my five year old grandson Michael declared 'you are the best cooker in the world'!

Perhaps that accolade belongs to the Remoska?

Karina Havlů M.A.
Born in Prague, Czech Republic.

Graduate of the Charles University of Prague, the Faculty of Philosophy, Karina also studied film and television production at FAMU – the Academy of Performing Arts.

For a number of years she has been active as a translator from both English and Italian, translating plays from the English language – Murray Schisgal 'We are a family', Neil Simon's 'Jake's Women', and a number of books both for adults and children.

She has concentrated particularly on biographies of world famous personages such as Sophia Loren 'Women and Beauty', Tom Hanks 'Journey to Stardom', from Italian the autobiography of Claudia Cardinale and the Memories of Fabrizio Ciano, the grandson of Mussolini.

Apart from her literary interest Karina is an ardent cook. Having lived a number of years in Rome and frequently returning there, in 1998 she published from personal practical experience her Italian Cookbook. She has published nearly twenty other cookery books, some of which have been translated. Her book on Macrobiotic Cookery was published in 2001 in Lithuania. In 2002 Karina published the very comprehensive Big Household Cookery book, which was also published in the same year in Slovakia.

Her book 'Varime v Remosce' – Cooking in the Remoska, was first published in 1997. Revised in 2001, some of these recipes now feature in this book together with others by Milena Grenfell-Baines who, like Karina Havlů was also born in Prague.

Dedication

For Michelle Kershaw
Customer Director
Lakeland Limited

Because you came to Prague!

Michelle and Anthony's favourite nibbles

Anthony's Roasted Pistachio and Pine Kernels. Shallow pan

1 tbsp olive oil,
100 g (4 oz) pistachio kernels
100 g (4 oz) pine nuts kernels
Black pepper
Salt

Heat the oil in the Remoska until hot but not smoking.
Add pistachio kernels and stir quickly until coated with oil.
Replace lid and cook for about 3–4 minutes.
Add pine nut kernels and stir until coated with oil and
well mixed in with pistachios.
Continue to cook until pine nuts take on a golden complexion.
Remove nuts from the pan and drain on absorbent kitchen paper.
Season with salt and black pepper to taste.

Variation
Use olive oil flavoured with chilli or season with salt and chilli.

All about the Remoska

'Good old Remoska', is there anyone who hasn't heard of it.... Sadly many of us have already forgotten about it, mother's or grandmother's is gathering dust in the attic, our kitchens are equipped with the latest electronic gadgets...from Karina Havlu's 'Cooking with the Remoska'.

There is no doubt that here in the UK – as elsewhere – today's modern ovens and microwaves, 'ready to cook' prepared recipes, the 'takeaways' and frozen food has changed our attitude to cookery. It is difficult to believe that after all the available computerised gadgetry this simple electric mini oven, the Remoska, invented in Czechoslovakia just after World War 2, was about to make a come-back. It is the simplicity of its design and the ease of cooking methods which is exactly the reason for its appeal.

It was manufactured quite extensively during the 40 years of Communist rule – it was cheap, efficient and in most people's small kitchens often replaced the oven.

Once liberated from the oppressive Communist regime, modern electric cookery aids available to Western Europe were being imported and the Remoska relegated to a dark corner of some kitchen cupboard.

However, people with small apartments, country cottages, caravans, boats and the like were slowly reminded that here was a mini oven in which mother and grandmother cooked very tasty dishes, had extolled its economic use of electricity (500W) and slowly the Remoska was once more in demand. Though the factory was still in production it was, through lack of investment, rundown and for sale.

In 1990, two enterprising young men Jiri Blazek and Jaroslav Ulicnik put all their resources and borrowings together to purchase the existing tools and machinery, moved the equipment to eastern Moravia where employment was needed and production began once again, mainly for the Czech market.

In 1999 I was visiting my cousin Helen in Prague. Before leaving, I bought her, as a parting present, a new Remoska to replace the one Helen's mother had been using for the past 40 years. Back in England, re-reading the promotional literature I was prompted to phone the factory and ask why had this mini oven never been exported abroad. Speaking to a complete stranger, before any names were given, the reply came, "paní, vy jste andel z nebe", we were speaking in Czech, Mr Ivo Svoboda, the marketing manager, for that is who it was, said – "lady, you are an angel from heaven…"

From that delightful encounter has grown a firm friendship. When I showed the Remoska to my friend Michelle Kershaw, Customer Director of Lakeland Limited, Michelle said "Let me take one home, I'll have a play with it".

Now, thanks to Michelle who was so impressed with the Remoska and Lakeland Limited, who import the Remoska to the UK, the little factory has doubled its output and its workforce.

Becoming one of Lakeland Limited's best sellers there are now over 35,000 Remoskas out there in the field, it was time to talk 'recipes'. Karina's book, 'Cooking with the Remoska' had been given to me, we met and now we have a good number of both translated and other tried and tested recipes from the UK in this book for you to enjoy.

Milena Grenfell-Baines

The Remoska

If you've bought this book, the
chances are you already own a
Remoska! If you don't, go out
and buy one! It is so versatile.

It is an electric mini oven with a lid that
does the cooking. Apart from the lid it
consists of Teflon lined pan and a stand.
The Remoska comes in two sizes, Grand
and Standard. A shallow pan is also available
in both sizes and recommended. Most of the recipes given here are for
the Standard size. It has a simple on/off switch, no graded heat control and
yet it cooks just like, if not better than an oven and is amazingly economical
with your electricity.

The Remoska is not a 'slow cooker'. On the contrary, some food will cook faster
than in a normal oven. When frying, have patience. Each time you take the lid off
you remove the source of heat so don't be tempted to take the lid off until you
see through the glass window the frying is done or the right colour achieved.

When ingredients in a recipe first need 'browning' or 'sealing' although this may
be done in the Remoska you may find it quicker using a frying pan.

Using the deep pan you may place your food in ovenproof dishes to fit in the
Remoska or directly in the pan. It may be used as a 'Bain Marie', heating food,
defrosting food (if you don't have a microwave) and it probably cooks the best
roast chicken you have ever tasted.

It works just like an oven. In it you may roast, braise, and bake sweet or savoury
food, casserole, and even fry. You can make toasted sandwiches, or cook ready
meals in foil containers. Ideal if you are on a fat free diet, you may wrap portions
of food in very lightly greased foil – fish particularly remains moist and flavour-
some. In principle, it is possible to prepare a whole meal for the family without
using the oven.

Puff pastry rises like a dream and sponge cakes stay moist.

Some general tips before beginning

All recipes in this book serve three to four people.

The recipes should be cooked in the Standard Remoska using the deep pan.

You can use the Grand Remoska , for bigger meals serving between six to eight people, adjusting ingredients and cooking times accordingly.

There is also a shallow pan available for both the Standard and the Grand Remoska which can be used for frying or to speed up the cooking process.

Once you have mastered the basic methods you will find you can adapt so many recipes and invent your own.

It is extremely economical to use, easy to clean – the Teflon base is non-stick so will rinse out – not even worth putting in the dishwasher though it's quite safe to do so.

To clean the lid, switch off, unplug from mains and when cool wipe the glass with a damp cloth. **Never immerse the lid in water.** When in use, if you need to remove the lid to stir, place it away from you upside down – **remember, it is the lid that does the cooking – and like opening an oven door – it will be hot.**

Do not heat the empty Remoska. Food, including cakes may be cooked from cold. As with all Teflon lined cooking pans, excess heating of an empty pan will damage the lining.

Some of the savoury recipes suggest they be served together with Czech dumplings. These cannot be made in the Remoska and to find out exactly how good they are for mopping up the various sauces we suggest a trip to Prague – (and if you wish, we can arrange a lesson from a friendly chef on how to make them). However, potatoes, rice or pasta will do very well as a replacement.

In a number of the meat recipes you will find caraway seed, marjoram and paprika, all very popular ingredients in Eastern Europe. A word about paprika. There is sweet paprika and 'sharp' paprika. Our advice is to use the sweet.

'Larding' is also suggested several times. This means that you make incisions into the meat with a sharp knife, about a centimetre across and 2–3 centimeters deep and insert strips of – usually bacon – about the thickness of your little finger.

The vinegar in the Czech Republic is diluted acetic acid found in the UK as 'Non-brewed Condiment' in most supermarkets. This lends itself better to 'souring' some of the dishes like cabbage.

Oil, unless specified is cooking oil of your choice. Although amounts are given you will find with use and practice less oil will suffice due to the non-stick Teflon lining of the pan.

Frying takes longer for the oil to get hot than in a standard fry pan but the result is really crisp on the outside, soft inside, no spluttering fat and no smell. If dieting you may cook without fat altogether.

When baking cakes, because the edges will bake slightly quicker than the centre, cut a disc of foil or the Magic Non-Stick Liner (Lakeland Catalogue Ref 5570) about the same diameter as the pan, then cut a hole in the centre about the diameter of a coffee mug. Place this disc over the baking cake for the last 15 minutes.

Cakes may be baked directly in the Remoska, or the pan lined with foil or a loose-based 18 cm (7 in) cake tin.

All flour in the recipes is plain.

Our grateful thanks to Teflon/Dupont for helping to sponsor the production of this book.

Teflon was discovered in 1938 when a young chemist by the name of Roy Plunkett working in the laboratory of an American firm Du Pont in New Jersey discovered a synthetic material with a very slippery surface. Since then, more than a billion pieces of kitchenware alone, covered with this 'slippery surface' have been sold the world over.

Conversion table never mix metric and imperial measurements

metric	imperial	metric	imperial	USA cups
15 g	¹/₂ oz	50 ml	2 fl oz	¹/₄
25 g	1 oz	75 ml	3 fl oz	
40 g	1 ¹/₂ oz	100 ml	4 fl oz	¹/₂
50 g	2 oz	150 ml	5 fl oz	
75 g	3 oz	175 ml	6 fl oz	
100 g	4 oz	200 ml	7 fl oz	
125 g	5 oz	250 ml	8 fl oz	1 cup
175 g	6 oz	275 ml	10 fl oz	1 ¹/₄ cups
200 g	7 oz	400 ml	14 fl oz	
225 g	8 oz	425 ml	15 fl oz	2 cups
250 g	9 oz	450 ml	16 fl oz	
300 g	10 oz	500 ml	1 pt	4 cups
350 g	12 oz	1 Litre	32 fl oz	
400 g	14 oz			
500 g	16 oz			
700 g	1 ¹/₂ lb			
900 g	2 lb			
2.5k g	5 lb			

> Conversions are approximate and have been rounded up or down. Follow one set of measurements only – do not mix metric and imperial measurements in one recipe.

Cooking times

Remember cooking in the Remoska is not an exact science. Times for cooking will vary depending on the contents i.e how thick your meat and how finely you chop other ingredients etc.

Times given in the recipes are for your guideline. You'll soon see how easy it is. It won't be long before you will be preparing all sorts of delicous offerings.

We would love to hear from you. If you have any comments, thoughts or new recipes you would like to share, contact us on our website –
www.hoorayforhomecooking.com
where you'll find other recipes, tips and discussion pages.

Starters

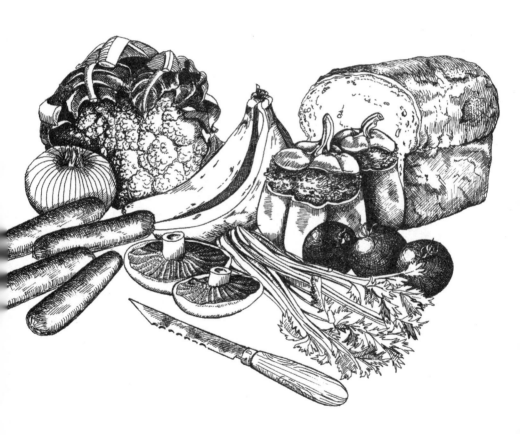

Contents in this section

Aubergine 'Schnitzels'

Best made in the shallow pan

*Frying oil to fill one third of
the Remoska*

2 firm large aubergines

Salt

*225 g (8 oz) plain flour
seasoned with salt and freshly
ground black pepper*

3 beaten eggs–maybe more

*500 g (1 lb) dried white
breadcrumbs*

2 lemons

A great favourite with the Grenfell-Baines
household and any guest who is lucky enough
to get to the plate first.

Slice aubergines 4 mm ($^1/4$ in) at a slight angle,
sprinkle the slices with salt and leave for 30 minutes. Rinse and pat dry. Put the flour in a plastic
bag, drop in slices of aubergine a few at a time,
shake the bag, dip the floured pieces in egg and
breadcrumbs and place on a baking tray, you
may need to separate the layers with baking
parchment. Heat the oil in the Remoska and
when really hot place four or five slices of
aubergine in the pan and leave to fry. Keep
an eye on the colour, when pale gold turn
the slices over, fry a little longer and place
on kitchen paper to drain residual fat.

Banana Kebabs with Bacon

4 firm bananas

100 g (4 oz) bacon rashers

A sprinkling of dried rosemary

Pour boiling water over unpeeled bananas
and wait until they turn lightly brown. This will
keep bananas from turning black during baking.
Peel and cut into 4 cm (2 in) long pieces, wrap
each in half a bacon rasher and place on skewer.
Arrange in the Remoska, sprinkle with rosemary
and bake on all sides, approx 15 minutes.

Serve warm.

Baked Stuffed Aubergine

2 medium aubergine
3 tbsp oil
I onion, finely chopped
I medium courgette
Salt and freshly ground
black pepper
225 g (8 oz) cooked chicken
50 g (2 oz) Gruyere cheese,
grated
I egg
I heaped tsp dried marjoram
275 ml (10 fl oz) tomato
juice

Cut washed aubergine in half lengthwise; scoop out the flesh taking care not to break the skin and dice. Gently poach empty skins in lightly salted water for five minutes, drain and dry.

Heat two tablespoons of the oil in a frying pan and fry the onion until translucent, add diced courgette and flesh of the aubergine. Lightly season and cook for another ten minutes, stirring occasionally. Stir in diced chicken, grated cheese, egg and marjoram. Fill the aubergine shells with this mixture. Place in the Remoska; drizzle with tomato juice mixed with one tablespoon of oil and bake for approx 25 minutes.

Serve with boiled potatoes, rice or fresh bread.

Baked Stuffed Mushrooms

4 large flat mushroom caps
50 g (2 oz) ham or
ham salami
50 g (2 oz) Gruyere cheese,
grated
I tbsp of chopped parsley or
chives
I garlic clove
Salt and freshly ground
black pepper
Butter for Remoska
50 g (2 oz) butter

Trim off mushroom stems, chop these finely and combine with finely cubed ham, grated cheese, parsley or chives and crushed garlic. Season and stuff mushroom caps with the mixture. Place in buttered Remoska, dot each cap with butter, cover with Remoska lid. Bake approx 20 minutes, until the mushrooms soften and are lightly brown.

Baked Stuffed Peppers

2 onions or leeks
3 garlic cloves
2 tbsp oil
500 g (1 lb) of mince meat
(pork, beef, chicken)
150 ml (5 fl oz) chicken stock
1 egg
1 tbsp fresh breadcrumbs
2 tbsp semolina
Pinch of grated nutmeg
Few drops Worcestershire
Sauce
1 tsp dried oregano or
marjoram
4 tbsp chopped parsley
Salt and freshly ground
black pepper
4 firm (and preferably
different coloured) peppers
50 g (2 oz) bacon
4 heaped tbsp tomato purée

In a large pan fry finely chopped onions or leeks and crushed cloves of garlic in oil and cook until translucent, add meat and brown quickly, stirring occasionally. Add stock and simmer until meat is soft and any liquid totally absorbed. Cool, then add the whisked egg, breadcrumbs, semolina, nutmeg, Worcestershire sauce, oregano or marjoram, parsley and season.

Slice tops off the peppers, scoop out seeds and pith from the inside and fill with meat mixture. Place diced bacon on the bottom of the Remoska, sit peppers on the bacon, drizzle with tomato purée thinned with a tablespoon of warm water. Bake approx 30 minutes. The peppers should remain slightly crunchy.

Serve with boiled potatoes, rice or bread.

Baked Tomatoes

Butter for Remoska
500 g (1 lb) tomatoes, sliced
1 garlic clove, crushed
2 onions, finely chopped
1 tbsp chopped fresh basil
Salt and freshly ground
black pepper
50 g (2 oz) fresh breadcrumbs
25 g (1 oz) butter

Butter the Remoska and place the tomato slices in together with the garlic. Mix together the onions and basil, spread over the tomatoes and season. Sprinkle with breadcrumbs and drizzle with melted butter. Cover and bake for approx 15–20 minutes until the breadcrumbs are pale gold.

Celeriac Sticks

225 g (8 oz) celeriac
50 g (2 oz) plain flour
50 g (2 oz) fine semolina
225 g (8 oz) Swiss cheese or
hard smoked cheese
75 g (3 oz) butter
Salt and freshly ground
black pepper
1 egg
Oil for Remoska

Grate celeriac, mix with sifted plain flour, semolina and grated cheese. Add softened butter, pinch of salt and knead into firm dough. Roll out thinly on plain floured surface. Cut into long fingers, brush with beaten egg, season lightly and arrange in oiled Remoska. Cover and bake until golden brown, approx 10–15 minutes.

Cod in Scallop Shells

700 g (1 1/2 lb) cod steak
Juice of 1 lemon
Salt
Butter for the Remoska
1/2 cucumber
Freshly ground black pepper
1 tbsp chopped parsley, mint
and chives, mixed
1 tsp white wine vinegar
1 tbsp boiling water
4 tbsp thick mayonnaise
Lettuce leaves
12 anchovy fillets

Dry the fish well, sprinkle with lemon juice and salt and leave in a cool place for 30 minutes. Butter the Remoska pan generously, place the fish in the pan, add an extra squeeze of lemon juice and cover with buttered paper. Cover and cook for approx 15 –20 minutes depending on the thickness of the fish. When cooked remove from the pan and leave to cool.

Peel the cucumber and cut into very small dice or roughly grate. Place in a colander, salt lightly, cover with a plate and leave to drain for 30 minutes. Place in a bowl, season with ground black pepper, sprinkle with the wine vinegar and the mixed herbs.

Whisk the boiling water into the mayonnaise. Take 6 scallop shells or small shallow bowls, line with lettuce leaves and a spoonful of the cucumber. When the fish is cold remove the skin and bones, carefully flake flesh with a fork. Spoon fish into the shells or bowls and coat with the mayonnaise. Decorate the tops with crossed anchovy fillets.

'Eggy' Bread with Cheese

2 eggs
100 g (4 oz) Gruyere cheese, grated
2 tbsp double cream
Salt and freshly ground black pepper
8 slices of French bread
Butter for Remoska
Chopped parsley

Beat eggs with cheese and cream and season. Dip bread slices in batter on both sides. Place in the buttered Remoska and bake until golden brown.

Garnish with parsley. Drizzle, if you like it, with tomato ketchup.

Peppers, or Tomatoes, Stuffed with Tuna

225 g (8 oz) cooked rice
175 g (6 oz) canned tuna in its own juice, drained
4 tbsp chopped parsley
1 tsp capers
1 egg
Salt and freshly ground black pepper
1 tbsp vegetable oil
1 large onion
4 large peppers
100 ml (4 fl oz) chicken stock

Mix rice with tuna, parsley, capers, egg and season. Fry the finely chopped onion and stir into the mixed ingredients. Cut tops off the peppers and remove seeds and pith. Stuff with mixture.

Stand peppers in the Remoska, add stock and cook until tender, approx 30 minutes. Peppers should be crunchy, not overcooked.

Ricotta and Herb Stuffed Mushrooms

4 large open cap mushrooms
1 tbsp each of chopped fresh
tarragon, dill and flat leaf
parsley
½ tbsp chopped chives
225 g (8 oz) Ricotta cheese
3 tbsp Parmesan cheese,
grated
Salt and freshly ground
black pepper
2 tbsp olive oil

Cut the stalks off the mushrooms and chop finely. Together with all the herbs and the chives work into the Ricotta adding two tablespoons of the Parmesan. Season. Brush all sides of the mushrooms with olive oil. Stuff the mushrooms with cheese mixture, top with the rest of the Parmesan and drizzle with the rest of the olive oil. Place in the Remoska and bake for approx 15–20 minutes.

Ricotta Tart

For pastry
25 g (1 oz) butter
50 g (2 oz) lard
175 g (6 oz) plain flour
Pinch of salt
3 tbsp very cold water,
more or less

Filling
300 g (10 oz) Ricotta cheese
Salt and freshly ground
black pepper
3 med. size eggs
50 g (2 oz) smoked salmon
50 g (2 oz) Gruyère cheese
18 cm (7 in) flan ring

Rub the fats into the flour and salt and mix with the cold water to a firm dough. Place in the refrigerator whilst preparing the filling.

Cream the Ricotta and season. Beat the eggs and gradually add them to the cheese. Cut the salmon into shreds and mix carefully into the egg and cheese mixture. Line the Remoska with a circle of Magic Non–Stick Liner or greaseproof paper and place in the flan ring. Roll out the pastry and line the flan ring. Fill with the prepared mixture. Cut the Gruyère cheese into thin slices and lay these over the top of the filling. Cover and bake until golden-brown and crisp, approx 25 minutes.

Scrambled Eggs with Sausage

1 tbsp oil
225 g (8 oz) sausage
8 eggs
Salt and freshly ground
black pepper
Pinch of ground sweet paprika
Handful parsley or chives

Heat oil in the Remoska, add sliced sausage, brown on all sides and pour beaten lightly seasoned eggs over the top. Cover and allow mixture to set. Sprinkle with paprika and chopped parsley or chives.

Serve with bread or toast, pickled gherkins or green salad.

Variation – Eggs with bacon or ham may be prepared in a similar manner.

Toast with Cheese

25 g (1 oz) butter
100 g (4 oz) Gruyere cheese,
grated
1 tbsp cream
1 tsp mustard
Salt and freshly ground
black pepper
4 slices of white toast
2 large tomatoes
1 tsp caster sugar
Butter for Remoska
Chopped parsley or chives

In a small pan, melt butter, add cheese and allow to melt, stirring occasionally. Add cream, mustard, season and stir. Spread mixture over the toast, top with tomato slices, season and sprinkle with caster sugar.

Butter the Remoska, place the prepared toasts in the pan, (you may need to put in two at a time, depending on the size of the bread) cover and bake until tomatoes are cooked– approx ten minutes.

Garnish with parsley or chives.

Toast with Cheese and Beer

25g (1 oz) butter
100 ml (4 fl oz) dark beer
50 g (2 oz) Cheddar cheese,
grated
1 tsp ground sweet paprika
4 slices of French bread,
(toasted)
Butter for Remoska
Salt

In a small pan melt butter, add beer and when
it is warmed through, stir in grated cheese,
season lightly, add the paprika and allow to
thicken stirring occasionally. Spread toast with
cheese mixture, place in buttered Remoska
and bake to golden brown, approx ten minutes.

Toast with Cheese and Spring Onions

4 slices of French bread
(toasted)
1 garlic clove
Salt
4 spring onions
4 slices of cheese—Emmenthal
Butter for Remoska

Rub the toasted bread with garlic and season
with salt. Sprinkle generously with finely chopped
spring onion, cover with sliced cheese, place in
buttered Remoska and bake until cheese starts
to melt, approx ten minutes.

Serve with wedges of tomatoes sprinkled with
salt and drizzled with olive oil.

Toast Italian

4 slices of bread
Butter for Remoska
100 g (4 oz) Mozzarella
cheese
4 small tomatoes
8 anchovies, drained—or a
corresponding amount of
anchovy paste
1 tsp dried oregano
Salt and freshly ground
black pepper
1 tbsp of olive oil

Toast bread in toaster. Butter the Remoska.
Slice Mozzarella and tomatoes, cut anchovies
in half lengthwise. Top toast slices with tomatoes,
anchovies and Mozzarella, sprinkle with oregano
and season. Place in buttered Remoska. Drizzle
lightly with oil, cover and bake until Mozzarella
starts to melt, approx seven—ten minutes.

Toast with Salami

8 slices of French bread
100 g (4 oz) soft salami
100 g (4 oz) Cheddar cheese,
or your choice, grated
8 tsp ketchup
Butter for Remoska

Toast bread in toaster. Top with salami slices, cover with cheese, drizzle with ketchup. Place in the Remoska and toast to melt the cheese, approx ten minutes.

Toast with Smoked Salmon

50 g (2 oz) smoked salmon
2 tbsp butter
1 lemon–grated rind and juice
4 tbsp chopped parsley or chives
Freshly ground black pepper
8 slices of French bread
50 g (2 oz) Jarlsberg cheese,
or your choice, grated
Butter for Remoska

Cut salmon into small pieces and fork into the softened butter, add grated lemon rind, drizzle with lemon juice and add parsley or chives, pepper to taste and mix thoroughly. Toast bread in toaster. Top with prepared salmon mixture, sprinkle with cheese, place in the buttered Remoska and bake approx five–seven minutes and serve immediately. Repeat as required.

Toast with Tomatoes

4 slices of bread
Butter for Remoska
4 small tomatoes
4 basil leaves or 1 tsp dried herbs
1 tsp caster sugar
Salt and freshly ground black pepper
A few drops of olive oil

Toast bread in toaster. Butter the Remoska. Toss scalded, peeled and chopped tomatoes with chopped basil or dried herbs, caster sugar and season to taste. Heap mixture onto toast and bake for approx five–six minutes. Drizzle toast with olive oil before serving.

Variation – Spread toasted bread slices with crushed garlic and then top with tomato mixture.

Vegetables

Lentils, beans, and peas are classified as pulses.
Before using them for the following recipes prepare them
according to the package instruction or use a canned equivalent.

There are excellent Pizza Dough ready mixes in supermarkets or
your corner shops. Try Wright's Ciabatta bread mix, half the bag
will make enough dough for a pizza base in the Standard Remoska.

Supermarket shelves have a vast choice of tomato and other sauces
to which you may add your favourite toppings. The Remoska will
cook a 20 cm (8 in) pizza from frozen in eight–ten minutes.

There is a vast choice of fresh and dried pasta on the market.
Choose your favourite to suit the recipe.

Contents in this section

Asparagus Gratin

20 sprigs of fresh asparagus
5 thin slices of boiled ham
Salt and freshly ground
black pepper
100 g (4 oz) of Gruyere,
thinly sliced
50 g (2 oz) unsalted butter
500 ml (1 pt) Béchamel sauce
(see page 137)

Clean asparagus and cut off hard ends. Cook in boiling lightly salted water for ten minutes, drain on kitchen paper. Lay four sprigs of asparagus on each ham slice, season lightly, cover with sliced cheese, roll ham slices up and place in buttered Remoska. Dot with butter.

Spoon over the Béchamel sauce, cover and cook for approx 15 minutes for the sauce to heat through and lightly brown.

Aubergine and Mushroom Moussaka

500 g (1 lb) aubergine
150 ml (5 fl oz) tomato juice
2 tbsp oil
100 g (4 oz) onion, chopped
2 garlic cloves, crushed
350 g (12 oz) button
mushrooms, sliced
1 red pepper, seeded and
chopped
500 g (1 lb) tomatoes, scalded
peeled and chopped
1/2 tsp dried or 1 tsp chopped
fresh marjoram
1 bay leaf
3 eggs
300 ml (10 fl oz) natural
yoghurt
Salt and freshly ground
black pepper
50 g (2 oz) Cheddar cheese,
grated

Cut the aubergine into 5 mm (1/4 in) thick slices, sprinkle with salt and leave to stand for 30 minutes. Rinse and wipe dry. Poach the aubergine slices in the tomato juice for three minutes, remove with a slotted spoon and set aside. Heat oil in separate pan, fry the onion and garlic for two minutes stir in the mushrooms, pepper, tomatoes and any extra juice remaining in the pan used to poach the aubergine. Add marjoram with bay leaf, bring to boil and simmer for a further 20 minutes. Place a layer of aubergine in a lightly greased Remoska, top with a layer of the mushroom sauce, add remaining aubergine and finish with remaining sauce. In a jug beat together the eggs and yoghurt, season with pepper only and pour on top. Sprinkle with the grated cheese, cover and bake until top is golden brown, approx 30 minutes.

Baked Broccoli with Béchamel Sauce

500 g (1 lb) broccoli
275 ml (10 fl oz) Béchamel
sauce (see page 137)
Pinch of grated nutmeg
225 g (8 oz) frozen peas
2 carrots
2 tbsp chopped parsley
50 g (2 oz) Lancashire
cheese, grated
2 tbsp oil for Remoska

Divide rinsed broccoli into rosettes and boil
in a small amount of lightly salted water until
tender. Drain. Prepare Béchamel sauce, stir
in nutmeg, peas, finely grated carrots, parsley,
and cooked broccoli. Pour the mixture into the
oiled Remoska, sprinkle with grated cheese and
bake until cheese is golden brown, approx 20
minutes. Serve with boiled potatoes.

Baked Cauliflower with Meat

1 cauliflower, medium size
100 g (4 oz) fresh bread-
crumbs
1 tbsp butter
4 tbsp chopped parsley
3 tbsp milk
1 egg
350 g (12 oz) cooked minced
chicken, lamb or beef
Salt and freshly ground
black pepper
Pinch of nutmeg
Butter for Remoska
250 ml (8 fl oz) milk
2 eggs

Divide rinsed cauliflower into florettes, boil in
lightly salted water until half-tender and drain.
Fry breadcrumbs in butter until golden. Stir in
chopped parsley, three tablespoons of milk, one
beaten egg and the minced meat. Season, add
a pinch of nutmeg and mix well. Butter Remoska,
place half of cauliflower in the base, top with
meat mixture and another layer of cauliflower.
Whisk milk with eggs, lightly season, pour over
top and bake approx 25–30 minutes, or until
the eggs are set.

Baked Cauliflower with Walnuts

50 g (2 oz) Cheddar cheese, grated

2 egg yolks

250 ml (8 fl oz) Béchamel sauce (see page 137)

1 cauliflower about 700 g (1 1/2 lb)

Butter and dried breadcrumbs for coating the Remoska

50 g (2 oz) ground walnuts or hazel nuts

Stir grated cheese and egg yolks into warm Béchamel sauce. Divide rinsed cauliflower into rosettes and boil in lightly salted water until half-tender. Stir into Béchamel sauce. Butter the Remoska, coat base and sides with breadcrumbs, pour in cauliflower mixture, sprinkle with ground nuts and bake approx 15 minutes or until light brown.

Baked Eggs in Rolls

2 bread rolls

25 g (1 oz) butter

4 eggs

Salt and freshly ground black pepper

4 tbsp chopped parsley or chives

Butter for Remoska

Cut rolls in half, carefully scoop out insides, spread lightly with butter. Place in the buttered Remoska, break an egg into each, season and cover with lid. Bake until egg sets, approx five–seven minutes. Sprinkle rolls with chopped parsley or chives.

Variation – You may also top the set eggs with finely chopped ham or ham salami and grated cheese, replace the warm lid of the Remoska and leave for a few minutes for the cheese to melt.

Baked Eggs with Tomatoes and Lager

Butter for greasing Remoska

4 large tomatoes

8 eggs

100 g (4 oz) Cheddar cheese, mature, grated

100 ml (4 fl oz) lager

Salt and freshly ground black pepper

Slice tomatoes and layer them in the buttered Remoska. Beat eggs with cheese and beer, season and pour over tomatoes. Cover and bake until set, approx seven–ten minutes.

Serve with bread or boiled potatoes.

Baked Fennel with Smoked Meat

4 bulbs of fennel

Butter for Remoska

300 g (10 oz) sliced boiled smoked ham, or ham salami

300 g (10 oz) frozen peas, defrosted

250 ml (8 fl oz) Béchamel sauce (see page 137)

6 slices toasting cheese, Emmenthal

2 tbsp chopped parsley

Remove outer leaves from the fennel, halve, cut out hard centre cores, rinse and boil in lightly salted water until tender. Drain; slice into 1 cm (½ in) thick pieces and place some in the bottom of a buttered Remoska. Alternate layers of ham and fennel.

Stir peas into the Béchamel sauce, pour over fennel and ham and bake for 15 minutes. Cover with the slices of toasting cheese and parsley and bake again until top turns golden brown, approx ten minutes.

Serve with boiled potatoes.

Baked Flageolet Beans with Vegetables

2 carrots

1 stick of celery

350 g (12oz) broccoli

350 g (12oz) canned flageolet beans

Salt and freshly ground black pepper

Oil for Remoska

250 ml (8 fl oz) Béchamel sauce (see page 137)

Pinch of grated nutmeg

Grate carrots and finely slice the celery. Divide broccoli into florets and boil in salted water for five minutes. Combine beans, broccoli and grated vegetables, season lightly, and place mixture in the oiled Remoska. Pour over Béchamel sauce flavoured with nutmeg and bake approx 25-30 minutes.

Baked Frozen Vegetables with Chicken Wings

*1 packet 500 g (1 lb)
frozen mixed vegetables
Oil for pan
1 tsp of crumbled chicken
stock cube or 1 tsp dried
mixed herbs*

*500 g (1 lb) potatoes
Salt and freshly ground
black pepper
1 tsp caraway seed
10 chicken wings
1 tsp barbecue spice
1 tbsp oil*

Spread partially defrosted vegetables on the base of the oiled Remoska and sprinkle with stock cube or dried mixed herbs. Cover vegetables with thin slices of peeled potatoes, season and sprinkle lightly with caraway seed.

Cover potatoes with a layer of chicken wings, lightly seasoned with barbecue spice. Bake in the Remoska for approx 45 minutes or until vegetables are tender and wings turn golden brown.

Baked Leeks

*500 g (1 lb) leeks
Butter and breadcrumbs for
Remoska
3 eggs
100 ml (4 fl oz) double cream
225 g (8 oz) Cheddar cheese,
grated
Pinch of ground nutmeg
Salt and freshly ground
black pepper*

Boil the well washed leeks in lightly salted water until just tender. Drain and cut into short pieces, place in the Remoska coated with butter and breadcrumbs.

Mix eggs with cream, cheese, nutmeg, season and pour over leeks. Bake for approx 20 minutes.

Serve with boiled potatoes or fresh bread.

Baked Lentils with Mushrooms

225 g (8 oz) lentils
1 onion
2 large garlic cloves
1 tsp caraway seed
Oil for pan
175 g (6 oz) mushrooms
3 large tomatoes, scalded, peeled and chopped
1 tsp sweet ground paprika
4 tbsp chopped parsley
Salt and freshly ground black pepper
2 eggs
150 ml (5 fl oz) milk
1 tbsp oil
2 tbsp fresh breadcrumbs for coating pan and for sprinkling over dish

Pre-soak lentils according to instructions and boil until tender, adding salt after the lentils are cooked. Using a saucepan fry finely chopped onion, crushed garlic and caraway seed in oil until golden, add cleaned, sliced mushrooms and fry briefly. Stir in scalded, peeled and chopped tomatoes and cook another five minutes. Add lentils, paprika, parsley and season. Whisk the eggs with milk, add to the lentils and pour the mixture into oiled, breadcrumb-coated Remoska.

Sprinkle more breadcrumbs over the lentils and bake for approx 30 minutes.

Baked Lentils with Smoked Boiled Ham

350 g (12 oz) lentils
350 g (12 oz) smoked boiled ham
1 large leek
Salt and freshly ground black pepper
Oil for Remoska
275 ml (10 fl oz) of sour cream

Cook lentils according to instructions. Stir in cubed smoked ham, finely sliced cleaned leek and season. Pour into oiled Remoska. Pour sour cream over top and bake approx 30 minutes.

Serve with sauerkraut or chopped cabbage salad.

Baked Onions with Boiled Ham

6 equal size onions to fit the Remoska

250 ml (8 fl oz) Béchamel sauce (see page 137)

100 g (4 oz) boiled ham or ham salami

50 g (2 oz) Cheddar cheese, mature, grated

Fresh breadcrumbs for topping

50 g (2 oz) butter

Salt and freshly ground black pepper

Boil peeled onions in lightly salted water until tender and drain. Carefully scoop out centres and chop finely. Add to Béchamel sauce, stir in diced ham, grated cheese and season.

Fill onion shells with the mixture and place in the buttered Remoska. Top with breadcrumbs and dot with butter. Bake approx 10–15 minutes until top turns golden brown.

Serve with bread or as accompaniment to meat.

Baked Pasta with Broccoli

350 g (12 oz) broccoli

350 g (12 oz) short dry pasta cooked according to packet instruction

Olive oil for Remoska

275 ml (10 fl oz) double cream

50 g (2 oz) Gruyere cheese, or your choice, grated

Pinch of grated nutmeg

Salt and freshly ground black pepper

Rinse broccoli, cut into rosettes and boil in lightly salted water until half-tender. Stir drained broccoli into cooked and drained pasta, transfer to oiled Remoska, pour seasoned cream mixed with cheese and nutmeg over the pasta and bake until golden brown, approx 20 minutes.

Baked Pasta with Cauliflower and Tomatoes

500 g (1 lb) cauliflower
1 onion
2 tbsp olive oil
3 large ripe tomatoes
Pinch of dried oregano
*Salt and freshly ground
black pepper*
*350 g (12 oz) rigatoni or
other short dried pasta
cooked to packet instruction*

Butter for Remoska
250 ml (8 fl oz) double cream
1 egg
Grating of nutmeg

Separate the cauliflower into rosettes and boil
in lightly salted water until half-tender. In a pan
fry chopped onion in olive oil until translucent,
add drained cauliflower, scalded, peeled and
chopped tomatoes, oregano, season, and cook
briefly. Add the cooked and drained pasta.

Transfer mixture into the buttered Remoska,
pour cream beaten with egg, nutmeg and pinch
of salt over the cauliflower and bake for approx
20 minutes or until the contents begin to turn
golden brown.

Baked Pasta with Chicken

*225 g (8 oz) cooked
chicken meat*
*Salt and freshly ground
black pepper*
*225 g (8 oz) Pecorino or
other hard cheese of your
choice, grated*
*Few leaves of fresh basil or
1 tsp dried herbs*
*150 ml (5 fl oz) double
cream*
*350 g (12 oz) short dry
pasta cooked according
to packet instructions*
Olive oil for pan
Breadcrumbs for topping

Cube chicken meat, season, mix with grated
cheese and add chopped basil leaves or dried
herbs. Stir in the cream. Drain cooked pasta
well, stir in chicken mixture and transfer into
oiled Remoska, top with breadcrumbs and bake
until light golden brown, approx 20 minutes.

Baked Pasta with Courgette and Ham

1 large onion
2 tbsp olive oil
350 g (12 oz) courgettes
Salt and freshly ground black pepper
300 g (10 oz) short cut dried pasta cooked to packet instruction
225 g (8 oz) boiled ham, ham salami or other type of ham or smoked meat
250 ml (8 fl oz) Béchamel sauce (see page 137)
50 g (2 oz) Gruyere cheese, grated
50 g (2 oz) Parmesan cheese, freshly grated

In a large frying pan fry peeled, sliced onion in oil until translucent. Add sliced courgettes, season and continue to fry for a further five minutes. Stir in cooked pasta and cubed ham or ham salami together with the courgettes and onions, mix thoroughly and transfer to the Remoska. Cover with Béchamel sauce mixed with grated Gruyere. Bake until golden brown, approx 20–30 minutes.

Before serving, top individual portions with Parmesan cheese.

Baked Pasta with Frozen Mixed Vegetables

1 onion
2 tbsp oil
225 g (8 oz) garlic ham salami
225 g (8 oz) frozen mixed vegetables–defrosted
350 g (12 oz) short pasta cooked according to instructions on packet
150 ml (5 fl oz) double cream or milk
100 g (4 oz) Pecorino cheese, or your choice, grated
1 egg
Pinch of dried oregano or thyme or marjoram
4 tbsp chopped parsley
Salt and freshly ground black pepper

Fry finely chopped onion in oil in the Remoska, stir in cubed ham salami. Add vegetables, lightly season to taste, and cook for five minutes. Stir cooked pasta into the vegetable mixture, add cream, half the cheese, egg, herbs, parsley, season and bake until top is golden brown, approx 20 minutes. Offer the remaining cheese at the table.

Baked Pasta with Mushrooms

2 tbsp olive oil
1 onion, finely chopped
350 g (12 oz) mushrooms,
sliced
Salt and freshly ground
black pepper
350 g (12 oz) short dry
pasta cooked according
to packet instruction
250 ml (8 fl oz) Béchamel
sauce (see page 137)
50 g (2 oz) Pecorino cheese,
grated
Olive oil for pan

In a frying pan, fry onion in oil until translucent, add mushrooms, season and fry a further five minutes. Toss with cooked, drained pasta, transfer to oiled Remoska. Pour Béchamel sauce mixed with cheese over top and bake, approx 20 minutes.

Baked Rice with Frozen Vegetables and Salami

300 g (10 oz) Patna or long
grain rice
100 g (4 oz) soft salami
2 tbsp butter
250 g (9 oz) frozen vegetable
medley (carrots, peas, corn)
275 g (10 fl oz) milk
2 eggs
Salt and freshly ground
black pepper
2 tbsp chopped parsley
100 g (4 oz) Emmenthal
cheese, grated

Cook rice according to instructions. In Remoska fry salami in butter until golden, add partially defrosted vegetables, and when warmed through, add rice and the milk mixed with whisked eggs. Season and add chopped parsley. Level the top, sprinkle with grated cheese and bake until golden brown, approx 30 minutes.

Serve with salad.

Baked Soya Beans with Mushrooms

350 g (12 oz) soya beans
225 g (8 oz) mushrooms
2 onions
1 egg
1 tsp dried marjoram
Grating of nutmeg
Salt and freshly ground
black pepper
Oil for Remoska

Cook the soya beans according to instructions. Blend, but not too fine. Slice wiped mushrooms and stir into soya beans together with the finely chopped onions. Stir in remaining ingredients to make a thick mixture and season.

Pour into the oiled Remoska and bake approx 25 minutes.

Baked Tomatoes with Pasta

Butter for Remoska
4 large tomatoes
225 g (8 oz) leftover cooked
pasta
Salt and freshly ground
black pepper
75 g (3 oz) Gruyere cheese,
grated

Butter the Remoska. Cut tops off tomatoes, scoop out insides. Lightly season tomato cavities, turn the tomatoes over and leave to drain for ten minutes. Add scooped out tomato to pasta, season, and mix with 50 g (2 oz) of cheese; stuff the tomatoes and place in buttered Remoska. Sprinkle the rest of the cheese over the tomatoes, cover and bake approx 15 minutes until cheese melts and starts to brown.

Baked Vegetable Casserole

100 g (4 oz) bacon
3 large peppers, red,
yellow, green
4 tomatoes
Butter for Remoska
500 g (1 lb) of potatoes,
boiled
2 eggs
250 ml (8 fl oz) double cream
Salt and freshly ground
black pepper

Fry diced bacon in a pan, add cleaned peppers cut into strips and fry for five minutes stirring constantly. Add scalded, peeled and sliced tomatoes, season and cook for a further ten minutes.

Butter the Remoska, layer with half of peeled thinly sliced potatoes, the cooked vegetables and top with the other half of potatoes. Whisk eggs with the cream, season to taste and pour over the top. Cover and bake for approx 30–40 minutes until light golden brown.

Braised Lentils with Vegetables

300 g (10 oz) lentils
1 large carrot
1 large onion
2 tbsp vegetable oil
2 rashers of streaky bacon
500 g (1 lb) tomatoes
900 ml (1 1/2 pt) water
1 vegetable stock cube
Salt and freshly ground
black pepper

4 tbsp chopped parsley or
chives

Soak lentils according to instructions on the packet. In the Remoska fry finely grated carrot and finely chopped onion in oil until golden brown. Add cubed bacon, and fry for five minutes. Stir in scalded, peeled chopped tomatoes, the lentils, water in which they soaked and extra water made up to 900 ml (1 1/2 pt) and crumble in the stock cube. Cook until all the liquid has been absorbed. Season to taste.

Serve with parsley or chives sprinkled on each serving.

Braised Onions

500 g (1 lb) small onions
50 g (2 oz) butter
25 g (1 oz) demerara sugar
Salt and freshly ground
black pepper
4 tbsp vegetable stock

Peel onions, place in Remoska and dot them with butter; sprinkle with demerara sugar, season and pour stock round them. Cover with lid and bake for approx 45 minutes or until the onions are soft and lightly caramelised.

Cabbage Rolls with Mushrooms

6 large cabbage leaves
1 small onion
2 garlic cloves
1 tbsp oil
100 g (4 oz) fresh
mushrooms
100 g (4 oz) cooked rice
2 hard boiled eggs
4 tbsp chopped parsley
Salt and freshly ground
black pepper
275 ml (10 fl oz) vegetable
stock

Blanch large cabbage leaves in lightly salted boiling water, drain, dry and spread out on a clean tea towel. Cut away any hard core. In a frying pan fry chopped onion and garlic in oil until golden brown, add cleaned, sliced mushrooms, fry for five minutes and season. Mix cooled mushrooms with boiled rice, finely chopped eggs, chopped parsley and season. Divide mixture into 6 parts and place each on one cabbage leaf, roll up into a neat parcel and fasten with cotton. Place cabbage rolls in the Remoska, add stock and cook until cabbage is tender and lightly browned, approx 30 minutes.

Campers Eggs and Bacon baked in Croissants

2 croissants
1 tbsp corn oil
4 rashers of streaky bacon
4 eggs
Salt and freshly ground
black pepper

Cut croissants in half lengthways and hollow out. In the Remoska fry bacon slices in oil until just crisp. Remove bacon and place croissant halves in remaining fat. Press fried bacon into scooped out rolls, pour in beaten eggs and season. Cover and bake until eggs are set.

Variation – eggs may also be topped with grated cheese before baking. Instead of bacon, any other kind of soft salami or smoked meat may be used. When cooked, the croissants may be drizzled with ketchup.

Caramelised Onions

2 tbsp olive oil
4 large onions
2 tbsp granulated or
brown sugar
Salt and freshly ground
black pepper
Few drops of vinegar

Heat oil in the Remoska and add onions sliced into rings. Cook onions until soft, approx ten minutes, stirring occasionally and adding a very small amount of water if needed. Stir in the sugar, season and cook onion to lightly caramelise. Timing here is difficult, take a look after 15 minutes. Add vinegar to taste and serve as accompaniment to meat.

Cauliflower Gratin

Large cauliflower, approx
700 g (1 1/2 lb)
Salt and freshly ground
black pepper
25 g (1 oz) butter
100 g (4 oz) Gruyere cheese,
grated
500 ml (1 pt) Béchamel sauce
(see page 137)

Divide cauliflower into rosettes, rinse and boil in lightly salted water until just tender. Place in the buttered Remoska, season, stir Gruyere cheese into the Béchamel sauce, spoon over cauliflower, cover and cook for approx 15 minutes for the sauce to become light brown.

Celery with Bacon

1 head of celery
4 thin rashers of smoked streaky bacon, rinded
275 ml (10 fl oz) cheese sauce (see page 137)
25 g (1oz) Cheddar cheese, or your choice, grated

Cook celery in boiling water until tender. Drain well and divide into four bundles. Wrap a bacon rasher around each bundle and arrange in the Remoska. Pour over the sauce and sprinkle the extra cheese on top. Bake for approx 20–30 minutes.

Garnish
Tomato slices
Parsley

Serve garnished with tomato slices and parsley.

Cottage Courgettes

700 g (1 1/2 lb) courgettes
1 medium sized onion
4 tbsp oil
1 large tomato, scalded, peeled and chopped
175 g (6 oz) mushrooms, washed and sliced
100 g (4 oz) cottage cheese
Salt and freshly ground black pepper
50 g (2 oz) fresh white breadcrumbs
2 tbsp Cheddar cheese, grated

Slice courgettes fairly thickly. Peel and slice onion. Heat oil in frying pan and fry courgette slices in batches, turning them when they are lightly browned. Place three-quarters of fried courgettes in the Remoska, keep rest for top. Fry onions slowly in remaining fat to soften, add the tomato and mushroom and cook for further two minutes.

Stir in the cottage cheese with half the bread-crumbs. Season well and spoon over the cour-gettes. Place the remaining courgettes over the top, mix the rest of the breadcrumbs with grated cheese and sprinkle over the top. Cover and bake approx 15–20 minutes to pale gold. This is very good eaten cold.

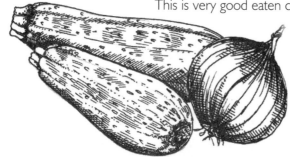

Frozen Spinach with Baked Eggs and Cheese

1 large onion
2 tbsp olive oil
1 packet 500 g (1 lb) frozen puréed spinach,defrosted
4 eggs
100 g (4 oz) grated cheese– your choice
Salt and freshly ground black pepper

In a frying pan fry finely chopped onion in olive oil until translucent, add spinach and cook until well heated through. Season and transfer to the Remoska. Smooth the spinach in the pan to make a flat surface, scoop out four hollows, and break an egg into each. Sprinkle with grated cheese, cover with lid and cook until the egg whites are set, approx ten minutes and the cheese begins to melt.

Serve with boiled potatoes.

Green Flageolet Bean Ring

1 large onion
25 g (1 oz) butter
1 vegetable stock cube
350 g (12 oz) frozen flageolet beans–defrosted
100 ml (4 fl oz) water
1 tsp dried marjoram
Salt and freshly ground black pepper
4 eggs
3 tbsp Edam cheese, grated
2 tbsp breadcrumbs for thickening
Pinch of nutmeg
Butter and breadcrumbs for coating the ring mould
A ring mould–21 cm (8 in) diameter.

Using a saucepan fry finely chopped onion in butter until translucent, crumble in the stock cube, add flageolet beans with water and simmer until tender. Let the water boil off, season the beans with marjoram, salt and pepper and leave to cool. Add whisked eggs, cheese, breadcrumbs and a pinch of nutmeg, mix well and pour the entire mixture into the buttered, breadcrumb-coated ring mould. Place in the Remoska, add water to come half way up the ring mould. Bake for approx 35–45 minutes.

Turn out and serve warm with boiled potatoes or serve chilled with fresh bread and salad.

Milena's tip
To protect the Remoska from being scratched line with a circle of 'Magic Non-stick Liner'.

Leek Parcels

6 medium sized leeks
50 g (2 oz) butter
1 large garlic clove, crushed
Salt and freshly ground
black pepper
3 pieces of aluminium foil

Cut the leeks in half and slice lengthways without cutting all the way through the leaves, to make a 'pocket'. Rinse thoroughly.

Mix butter, crushed garlic and a pinch of salt and spread into leek leaves. Wrap two leeks together in foil, seal tightly to keep juice from escaping and place the three parcels in the Remoska.

Bake approx 20–25 minutes. Serve with bread or boiled buttered potatoes.

Milena's tip
If you thickly slice two large washed unpeeled potatoes and a large peeled parsnip, place them in the Remoska with a little oil and seasoning, start cooking and after ten minutes sit the foil parcels on top, you will have a complete meal in the given time.

Mushroom Goulash

2 tbsp vegetable oil
2 onions
2 tsp sweet paprika
1 tsp caraway seed
500 g (1 lb) fresh
mushrooms
1 level tbsp plain flour
2 red peppers
4 tomatoes
200 ml (7 fl oz) mushroom
stock (cube)
Salt and freshly ground
black pepper
1 tbsp of sour cream
Juice of 1/2 lemon

In the Remoska fry finely sliced onions in oil until translucent. Stir in sweet paprika, caraway seed, sliced mushrooms, sprinkle with flour, stir, cover and fry for 5 minutes. Add cleaned, finely sliced peppers, scalded, peeled and chopped tomatoes and the stock. Season, cover with lid and cook until soft, approx 20 minutes. When ready, stir in the sour cream and the lemon juice.

Serve with bread or boiled potatoes.

Piperade

*1 each of red, green and
yellow peppers*
2 tbsp olive oil
2 garlic cloves, finely sliced
5 large eggs
*Salt and freshly ground
black pepper*
*Handful of flat leaf parsley,
chopped*

Core and seed the peppers and cut them into
strips about 1 cm (½ in) wide. Heat the oil in
the Remoska and fry peppers until they soften.
Add the garlic and cook a further five minutes.
Stir occasionally.

Whisk up the eggs and season. Pour the eggs
into the Remoska, stir gently to allow the eggs
to seep to the bottom of the pan. Replace the
lid and cook until the eggs are set, approx ten
minutes. Sprinkle with parsley.

Eat hot, cold or cooled stuffed into fresh French
baguette and take on picnic.

Red Onion and Blue Cheese 'Tarte Tatin'

*6 red onions peeled and cut
in half horizontally or as
many as will fit into the base
of the Remoska*

75 g (3 oz) butter
1 tbsp oil
*1 tbsp fresh chopped thyme
or 2 tsp dried thyme*
100 g (4 oz) Stilton or Danish Blue cheese
1 pack ready rolled puff pastry

In the Remoska fry onions in butter and oil until
translucent. Add thyme, stir and leave to cool.
Arrange the onions with cut side down. Crumble
cheese over the onions. Cut out pastry slightly
larger than the circumference of the pan, prick
all over, cover the onions and tuck the pastry
well down the sides.

Bake for 20 minutes or when you see the
pastry crispy, risen and golden brown. Allow
to cool a little, take a plate that will fit over
the pastry and carefully turn out so the onions
are uppermost.

Red Peppers stuffed with Fennel

Use the Grand Remoska – halve quantities for the Standard Remoska

5 tbsp oil
4 fennel bulbs
4 large red sweet peppers
2 onions, finely chopped
3 garlic cloves
2 x 225 g (8 oz) tubs Ricotta cheese
50 g (2 oz) shelled pistachios, finely chopped
350 g (12 oz) canned chopped plum tomatoes
150 ml (5 fl oz) water
1 tbsp tomato purée
1 tsp sugar
Large pinch of cayenne pepper
1 tbsp flat leaf parsley, finely chopped
Salt and freshly ground black pepper

Try to buy peppers and fennel bulbs of uniform size so that the trimmed fennel bulbs will just fit inside the halved peppers.

Grease the Remoska with 1 tablespoonful of oil. Halve the fennel bulbs lengthwise and trim them, discarding the woody cores and reserving the leafy tops. Blanch the bulb halves for five minutes in boiling water. Drain and pat dry, halve the peppers lengthwise and remove all seeds and pith. Heat three tablespoons of the oil in a frying pan and gently fry the onions and two of the chopped cloves of garlic until just translucent. Cool.

In a bowl mix the cooled onion/garlic into the Ricotta together with nuts and seasoning. Place three or four spoonfuls of this mixture in each of the pepper halves. Carefully place a blanched fennel bulb in each pepper half so that it sits on the cheese mixture. Add more mixture around the edges to fill if necessary. Transfer the peppers to the Remoska.

Mix canned tomatoes and their liquid with the warm water, the tomato purée, sugar, remaining chopped garlic, cayenne, parsley and salt to taste. Pour this carefully around the stuffed peppers. Drizzle remaining oil over the tops of the stuffed peppers, cover and bake for approx 30–40 minutes until the cheese is bubbling and the peppers are beginning to go brown. Garnish with the fennel sprigs.

Serve hot or at room temperature as part of a buffet or as a starter.

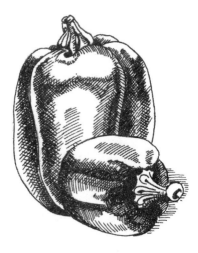

Roasted Peppers with Anchovies and Goats Cheese

2 large red peppers
3 tbsp extra virgin olive oil
225 g (8 oz) goats cheese log
100 g (4 oz) anchovy fillets in oil, drained
Bunch of fresh basil, shredded
Salt and freshly ground black pepper
Pitta bread

Cut peppers in half, remove seeds and pith. Place peppers in the Remoska, drizzle with oil and bake long enough to soften, approx 20 minutes. Cool a little, remove from the Remoska, crumble cheese into each pepper, season, drizzle with more olive oil, replace, close the lid and cook long enough to melt the cheese, approx 10–15 minutes.

Arrange the anchovy fillets over the peppers, sprinkle with the basil.

Serve with toasted or grilled pitta bread.

Roasted Vegetables

2 carrots
4 large potatoes
2 onions
3 leeks
Butter for Remoska
Salt and freshly ground black pepper
125 g (5 oz) red Cheddar cheese, grated
275 ml (10 fl oz) milk
2 tbsp double cream

Slice rinsed carrots, peeled potatoes, chop the onions finely and finely slice the leeks. Place onions in the buttered Remoska, then a layer of potatoes, carrots and finally the leeks. Season each layer, sprinkle on some of the cheese and drizzle with half of the milk mixed with cream. Top final layer with cheese, drizzle with the rest of the milk/cream mix and bake in the Remoska approx 45 minutes until crispy and golden brown.

Variation – Two or three rashers of thinly cut smoked streaky bacon sliced up or 'lardons' available in most supermarkets, stirred in with the vegetables produce a great appetizing aroma and flavour.

Spinach Burgers

1 onion
1 tbsp oil
300 g (10 oz) frozen chopped spinach–defrosted
Salt and freshly ground black pepper
2 whole-wheat rolls or bread-crumbs for thickening
150 ml (5 fl oz) milk
1 egg
100 g (4 oz) Gruyere cheese, or your choice, grated
Oil for shallow frying

In a frying pan, fry chopped onion in one table-spoon of oil until translucent, add defrosted spinach, season to taste and allow excess liquid to cook off. Transfer to a mixing bowl. Dice the bread rolls and moisten with milk. Stir into cooled spinach; add egg and grated cheese. Form burgers from mixture and fry in hot oil in the Remoska until golden brown. If the mix is too sloppy add more breadcrumbs.

Serve with mayonnaise or ketchup and potatoes prepared according to your choice.

You may, of course fry the burgers in the frying pan while the Remoska is baking a creamy potato and onion gratin.

Tofu Burgers

1 onion
1 tbsp oil
350 g (12 oz) Tofu
1 egg
2 tbsp Cheddar cheese, grated
4 tbsp fresh breadcrumbs
2 tbsp chopped parsley
1/2 tsp dried marjoram
Salt and freshly ground black pepper
Oil for frying

In a frying pan fry finely chopped onion, cool, crumble in Tofu, the whisked egg, cheese, breadcrumbs, parsley and marjoram. Lightly season, form into small burgers and fry on both sides in oil in the Remoska.

Serve with potatoes prepared according to taste or bread and various sauces.

Tofu Slices

350 g (12 oz) Tofu
Salt
Plain flour
1 egg
Breadcrumbs
Oil for frying

Cut Tofu into thin slices, lightly season, dust with plain flour, dip in beaten egg and coat with breadcrumbs. Fry on both sides in hot oil in the Remoska until golden brown. Serve with boiled or mashed potatoes and salad or freshly cooked vegetables.

You could fry the Tofu slices in a normal frying pan whilst using the Remoska for baking sliced potatoes over which you could drizzle a little olive oil, add a few spikes of rosemary, slices of garlic, salt and pepper. For this a shallow pan would be ideal.

Tomatoes and Peppers with Egg and Smoked Meat

1 tbsp oil
225 g (8 oz) smoked meat
(soft salami, sausages,
boiled smoked ham etc.)
1 onion
2 peppers
3 tomatoes
Salt and freshly ground
black pepper
6 eggs

Add oil to the Remoska; add sliced smoked meat and brown on all sides. Add finely chopped onion and fry briefly. Stir in very finely sliced peppers, scalded, peeled and diced tomatoes, season and cook for five minutes. Finally stir in whisked eggs, cover and allow to just set.

Serve with fresh bread, rolls or boiled potatoes.

Tomatoes stuffed with Pine Nuts

3 large tomatoes

Stuffing
2 tbsp olive oil
*1 medium sized onion,
peeled and finely chopped*
100 g (4 oz) pine nuts
*100 g (4 oz) soft whole
wheat breadcrumbs*

*1 garlic clove, peeled and
crushed with salt*
2 tbsp fresh chopped parsley
1 tbsp fresh or dried thyme
*Salt and freshly ground
black pepper*

Slice off tops of the tomatoes and scoop out the seeds. Sprinkle inside with salt and place upside down in a colander to drain while preparing the stuffing.

Heat the oil in a saucepan, fry onion until soft, remove from the heat and stir in pine nuts, breadcrumbs, garlic, parsley and thyme. Season to taste.

Fill tomato with nut mixture, replace tomato tops, stand in the lightly oiled Remoska and bake for approx 20–30 minutes.

Vegetable Curry

*350 g (12 oz) ripe tomatoes,
scalded, peeled and diced*
2 medium size courgettes
1 large carrot
2 medium size onions
2 garlic cloves
2 tbsp oil
*275 ml (10 fl oz) vegetable
stock*
1 tsp curry powder
1 small can of corn kernels
100 g (4 oz) pitted olives
*Salt and freshly ground
black pepper*
*Few leaves of fresh basil or
1 tsp dried*
4 tbsp chopped parsley

Scald, peel and dice tomatoes. Slice courgettes and carrots. Fry the chopped onion and crushed garlic in the Remoska until translucent. Add courgettes, carrots and vegetable stock. Cook for ten minutes or until vegetables soften, add diced tomatoes, curry powder to taste, season to taste and cook for a further ten minutes. Add drained corn, olives, chopped basil and heat through and add chopped parsley.

Serve with meat or poultry or as main course with bread, boiled potatoes or rice.

Vegetable Loaf Baked in Foil

500 g (1 lb) potatoes
1 tbsp oil
1 large onion
200 g (7 oz) frozen
spinach, defrosted
125 g (5 oz) frozen mixed
vegetables, peas, carrots,
corn, defrosted
Salt and freshly ground
black pepper
3 eggs
200 g (7 oz) Edam cheese,
grated
1–2 tsp dried marjoram
Pinch of nutmeg
Butter and breadcrumbs
for coating foil

Parboil unpeeled potatoes in lightly salted water, peel, cool and grate coarsely. In a saucepan heat oil, add finely chopped onion and cook until golden brown. Add spinach and vegetables, season lightly and simmer for a few minutes. Cool. Mix grated potatoes with the cooked vegetables; add beaten eggs, grated cheese, marjoram and nutmeg. Form mixture into a loaf. Wrap in buttered, breadcrumb-coated foil, pierce in a few places with a cocktail stick to allow steam to escape, place in the Remoska and bake for approx 40 minutes. Remove foil and cut loaf into slices.

Serve with fresh salad. The vegetable loaf may also be served chilled.

Vegetable Soufflé

350 g (12 oz) celeriac
1 carrot
1 small courgette
1 large onion
2 tbsp olive oil
4 eggs, separated
100 (4 oz) of cold, finely
diced cooked chicken or
boiled ham
100 g (4 oz) Cheddar cheese,
or your choice, grated
100 g (4 oz) plain flour
1/2 tsp baking powder
2 tbsp olive oil
Salt and freshly ground
black pepper
Butter and breadcrumbs for
coating the Remoska

Roughly grate peeled celeriac, carrot and courgette, finely chop the onion and stir-fry to lightly cook all these in a frying pan. Cool and add the egg yolks previously well whisked and the chosen diced meat, grated cheese, flour sifted with the baking powder, the oil and season. Mix thoroughly and fold in stiffly whisked egg whites. Pour the mixture into buttered, breadcrumb coated Remoska and bake until risen and golden brown, approx 30–40 minutes.

Serve soufflé with mashed potatoes and salad.

Vegetable Soufflé with Smoked Boiled Ham

225 g (8 oz) boiled smoked ham or ham salami

500 g (1 lb) of frozen mixed vegetables

150 ml (5 fl oz) double cream

3 eggs, separated

100 g (4 oz) Lancashire tasty cheese, or your choice, grated

Salt and freshly ground black pepper

Butter and breadcrumbs for coating Remoska

Cube smoked ham or salami, mix with partially defrosted vegetables, whisk up double cream with beaten egg yolks, add to vegetables with the cheese and season. Fold in stiffly beaten egg whites. Pour mixture into butter and breadcrumb coated Remoska and bake until golden brown approx 20 minutes.

Serve with boiled potatoes.

Potatoes

Contents in this section

Baked Mashed Potatoes

Butter for Remoska
350 g (12 oz) mashed
potatoes
1 large leek
100 g (4 oz)Cheddar cheese,
or your choice
50 g (2 oz) fresh breadcrumbs
2 tbsp butter, melted
Salt and freshly ground
black pepper

Butter the Remoska. Mix mashed potatoes
with finely sliced leek, grated cheese, season
to taste and spoon into Remoska. Sprinkle
with breadcrumbs, drizzle with butter and
bake until surface turns golden brown, approx
15–20 minutes.

Serve with cooked vegetables or green salad.

Baked Potatoes with Bacon

10 small even sized potatoes
Pinch of grated nutmeg
10 thin rashers of bacon
Oil for the Remoska
4 tbsp Cheddar, Lancashire
cheese, or your favourite,
grated
Freshly ground black pepper

Peel and parboil the potatoes in lightly salted
water. Drain, lightly sprinkle with nutmeg, wrap
in slices of bacon, securing each with a cocktail
stick. Place in the oiled Remoska, cover and bake
until the potatoes are soft, approx 30 minutes.
Sprinkle with the grated cheese, cover and cook
until golden brown. Serve with a mixed salad.

Baked Potatoes with Blue Cheese

Oil for the Remoska
3 large potatoes
50 g (2 oz) Stilton or Danish
Blue cheese, crumbled
2 large tomatoes
1 garlic clove
4 tbsp chopped parsley
1 tsp dried oregano
Salt and freshly ground
black pepper

Boil the potatoes in their skins until nearly soft in
lightly salted water. Cool slightly and cut lengthways, carefully scoop out the centre, and mix
with the grated cheese leaving a small amount
to sprinkle on the top. Scald, skin and chop the
tomatoes, stir in crushed garlic, parsley, oregano
and season. Place tomato mixture on the bottom of the oiled Remoska. Fill the scooped out
potato centres with the cheese/potato mix, sit
potato halves on top of tomatoes, cover and
bake for approx 15 minutes until cheese turns
golden brown.

Baked Potatoes with Garlic

3-4 large potatoes
2 garlic cloves
1 tsp of salt
2 tbsp olive oil
Salt and freshly
ground black pepper

Scrub, but do not peel the potatoes and slice thickly 5 mm ($\frac{1}{4}$ in). Crush the garlic with salt, place potatoes and garlic in the Remoska, drizzle with olive oil, season, stir, cover with lid and switch on. After 15 minutes give the potatoes a stir, replace lid and cook until golden brown, approx 30 minutes.

Now, here is where you may start ringing the changes. Add to the potatoes a large peeled and sliced sweet potato, sliced onion, a handful of sliced leeks, cupful of chopped smoked bacon, sprinkle with rosemary and when cooked, sprinkle with grated cheddar. Replace the lid and cook for a further seven–ten minutes.

Baked Potatoes with Horseradish and Sour Cream

3 large baking potatoes
3 egg yolks
150 ml (5 fl oz) sour cream
3–4 tbsp grated hot horseradish
1–2 tbsp fresh lemon juice
Salt and freshly ground
black pepper

Butter

Bake potatoes in the Remoska for approx one hour until soft. Whisk egg yolks, cream, horseradish and lemon juice in a large bowl. Cut potatoes in half and spoon insides into the bowl reserving the skins. Mash the potato, the sour cream and flavourings together, season with salt and a little pepper. Taste and add more horseradish and/or lemon juice if required. Pile the potatoes back into the skins, place back into the Remoska, dot the surface with butter and bake, approx 15–20 minutes until tops are brown.

Baked Potatoes with Mushrooms – I

500 g (1 lb) potatoes
350 g (12 oz) brown mushrooms
1 large onion
2 large garlic cloves
Salt and freshly ground black pepper
2 eggs
175 ml (6 fl oz) double cream
100 ml (4 fl oz) mushroom stock (cube)
Pinch of grated nutmeg

Layer peeled, finely sliced potatoes with cleaned thinly sliced mushrooms in the buttered Remoska. Top each layer with some finely sliced onion and crushed garlic, season and continue alternating layers until ingredients are used finishing with a layer of potatoes. Whisk eggs with cream, stock and add a pinch of nutmeg. Pour over the layered potatoes and mushrooms. Cover and bake until potatoes soften and brown, approx 30–40 minutes.

Baked Potatoes with Mushrooms –2

700 g (1 1/2 lb) potatoes
2 garlic cloves
1 tsp salt
Oil for the Remoska
225 g (8 oz) fresh mushrooms
3 tbsp olive oil
Salt and freshly ground black pepper

Slice the potatoes in equal fine slices 3 mm (1/8 in). Crush garlic with salt. Oil the Remoska. Layer half the potato slices in the Remoska, slice the mushrooms, layer these over the potatoes, drizzle with half the oil, layer the other half of the sliced potatoes over the mushrooms, drizzle with remaining oil and season. Cover and cook until potatoes and mushrooms are tender, approx 30 minutes.

Baked Potatoes with Tomatoes

500 g (1 lb) potatoes
Oil for Remoska
1 large onion
500 g (1 lb) tomatoes
Salt and freshly ground black pepper
Pinch of dried oregano or basil
3 tbsp fresh breadcrumbs
25 g (1 oz) butter

Cut well-scrubbed potatoes into thick slices 5 mm (1/4 in). Arrange half of them in a layer on the bottom of oiled Remoska. Cover with half of the sliced onion, half of the sliced tomatoes, season, sprinkle with oregano or basil. Repeat. Cover with breadcrumbs, drizzle with melted butter and bake until potatoes are tender and the top is golden brown and crisp, approx 30–40 minutes.

Baked Potatoes with Vegetables

500 g (1 lb) potatoes
200 g (7 oz) carrots
1 large onion
2 garlic cloves
Sprig of fresh or
1 tsp dried thyme
Dash of chilli powder
2 tbsp oil
Salt and freshly ground
black pepper
4 tbsp chopped parsley

Thinly slice the peeled potatoes and carrots. Roughly chop onion and finely chop the garlic. Combine in the Remoska with the thyme, chilli powder to taste, drizzle with oil, season and toss thoroughly. Cover with lid, bake and stir occasionally until tender, approx 30–40 minutes. Sprinkle with finely chopped parsley.

'Bramborák' Potato Pancakes

700 g (1 ½ lb) potatoes
100 g (4 oz) plain flour
2 eggs
3-5 garlic cloves
Salt and freshly ground
black pepper
1 tsp dried marjoram
Oil for shallow frying

Peel and grate potatoes and immediately stir in plain flour. Add beaten eggs, crushed garlic, marjoram and season to taste. Heat the oil in the Remoska and using a tablespoon form round pancakes and fry on both sides until golden brown.

Variations – add to the mixture finely cubed salami, boiled smoked ham or lightly cooked chopped mushrooms.

Fried Potato Croquettes

500 g (1 lb) potatoes
1 egg
75 g (3 oz) Stilton or Danish
Blue cheese, crumbled
Pinch of grated nutmeg
4 tbsp chopped parsley
1 tsp dried oregano
Salt and freshly ground
black pepper
Plain flour for coating
Oil for shallow frying

Boil unpeeled potatoes in lightly salted water until soft. Whilst hot, peel and mash. When cooled, stir in egg, blue cheese, pinch of nutmeg, chopped parsley, oregano, season and mix thoroughly. Form mixture into small croquettes, dust with plain flour. Pre-heat oil in Remoska and shallow fry on all sides until golden brown. Drain fried croquettes on paper towel. Serve with roast meat, poultry or vegetable dishes.

Janson's Temptation

Butter for Remoska
700 g (1 1/2lb) potatoes
2 large onions
1 tin anchovies drained,
save oil
25 g (1 oz) butter
Butter for greasing the pan
150 ml (5 fl oz) double cream
Salt and freshly ground
black pepper

Butter the Remoska. Peel and thinly slice potatoes and onions. Arrange half the potatoes on the bottom of Remoska, cover with onions mixed with finely chopped anchovy fillets. Add a little freshly ground pepper, cover with the rest of the potatoes, pour over the oil from drained anchovies, half the cream and dot with butter. Bake for 20 minutes, add the rest of the cream and bake for approx 15 minutes or until the potatoes are tender and a golden crust has formed on the surface.

Mashed Potatoes with Leeks

500 g (1 lb) potatoes
2 large leeks
1 dessertspoon of butter
75 ml (3 fl oz) milk
1 egg
2 tbsp double cream
50 g (2 oz) butter
Pinch of grated nutmeg
Salt and freshly ground
black pepper
50 g (2 oz) Cheddar cheese,
or similar, grated

Boil unpeeled potatoes in lightly salted water until soft. Peel whilst warm and either mash or sieve them. (Never mash potatoes in a food processor). Clean leeks, slice finely and gently cook in the butter. Warm milk to tepid, stir into mashed potatoes together with whisked egg, double cream, butter, cooked leeks, grated nutmeg and season. Butter the Remoska, add mashed potato and spread level. Sprinkle with grated cheese; cover and bake for approx 20–25 minutes until golden brown.

Serve with salad.

Milena's Potato Burgers

700 g (1 1/2 lb) potatoes
1 egg
1 yolk
3 tbsp Stilton or Danish Blue
cheese, crumbled
4 tbsp chopped parsley
Pinch of grated nutmeg
1 tsp dried marjoram
Salt and freshly ground
black pepper
Oil for shallow frying

Peel potatoes, cut into quarters. Boil in lightly salted water until soft. Drain and mash. Stir in egg, yolk, blue cheese, chopped parsley, nutmeg, marjoram, season and mix thoroughly. Using a spoon drop mounds of mixture into previously heated oil in the Remoska, lightly flatten the tops with the back of a spoon and fry on both sides until golden brown. Serve either with salad, or as accompaniment to meat, poultry or other dishes.

One Big Potato Cake!

1 medium onion
2 tbsp butter
500 g (1 lb) potatoes
Salt and freshly ground
black pepper
3 garlic cloves
1 tsp dried marjoram
1 tsp caraway seed
6 tbsp plain flour
Butter for Remoska

In a frying pan lightly fry finely chopped onion in the butter, stirring constantly. Grate peeled potatoes, season to taste, add the fried onion, crushed garlic, marjoram, caraway seed and plain flour. Stir thoroughly; pour the mixture into the buttered Remoska and bake until golden brown, approx 20–25 minutes.

Potato 'Gateau'

500 g (1 lb) potatoes
Butter for Remoska
125 g (5 oz) soft cream cheese, Quark or Ricotta
100 g (4 oz) mixed frozen vegetables
1 egg
50 g (2 oz) Cheddar cheese, or similar, grated
Salt and freshly ground black pepper
25 g (1 oz) melted butter
75 ml (3 fl oz) milk

Peel and finely slice potatoes 3 mm (¹/8 in). Butter the Remoska and cover the base with half the potato slices. Stir together cream cheese, defrosted vegetables, egg, two tablespoons of the grated cheese; season. Spread this mixture over the potatoes. Overlap remaining potatoes, brush with melted butter, pour over milk, cover with lid and bake until potatoes are tender, approx 30–35 minutes. Sprinkle remaining grated cheese over potatoes, cover and bake until golden brown, approx ten minutes.

Serve with a fresh tomato salad.

Potato Goulash with Lager

700 g (1¹/2 lb) potatoes
2 large onions
2 garlic cloves
2 tbsp oil
4 large tomatoes
2 tsp sweet ground paprika
275 ml (10 fl oz) lager
Salt and freshly ground black pepper
1 tsp dried marjoram
Fresh breadcrumbs as required

Peel and dice the potatoes. In the Remoska fry the finely chopped onion and garlic in the oil until transparent. Add scalded, peeled and chopped tomatoes (or use tinned tomatoes but drain some of the juice off first) cook for a few minutes, add the sweet paprika, diced potatoes and stir well. Add lager, season and add marjoram. Stir from time to time and cook until potatoes are soft, approx 25–30 minutes. If necessary, thicken the gravy with breadcrumbs.

Potatoes Baked with Onion

700 g (1 1/2 lb) potatoes
2 large onions
1 tsp caraway seed
275 ml (10 fl oz) double cream
Salt and freshly ground black pepper

Cut peeled potatoes into small cubes; coarsely chop the onions and toss together with caraway seed, season. Place in the Remoska, pour cream over the top and bake until potatoes are tender, approx 25–30 minutes.

Potatoes with Smoked Mackerel

500 g (1 lb) waxy potatoes
225 g (8 oz) smoked mackerel fillets
150 ml (5 fl oz) double cream
275 ml (10 fl oz) full cream milk
1 tbsp grain mustard
Salt and freshly ground black pepper

Peel and slice the potatoes 3 mm (1/8 in). Place in the Remoska. Break up the mackerel fillets and gently spoon them amongst the potatoes. Stir together the cream, milk, mustard and a little salt and pepper. Pour over the potatoes and bake until the cream is bubbling and the potatoes tender, approx 30 minutes.

Swiss Potatoes

4 large cold boiled peeled potatoes
2 tbsp vegetable oil
1 large onion
25 g (1 oz) butter
Salt and freshly ground black pepper

Grate potatoes coarsely. Heat oil in the Remoska and fry chopped onion until translucent. Add grated potatoes, stir, season, stir in butter, cover and bake until golden brown, approx 20 minutes. Serve as accompaniment to meat.

Stuffed peppers with fennel, recipe page 46

top Potato dishes, recipes page 55–62   *bottom* Toast starters, recipe page 23–26

Stuffed tomatoes, recipe page 21

top *Cauliflower gratin, recipe page 41*   *bottom* *Chicken drumsticks, recipe page 86*

Baked pasta with frozen mixed vegetables, recipe page 37

Duck breast, Chinese style, recipe page 94

Roast leg of lamb stuffed with plums, recipe page 67

Chicken, fried with vegetables, recipe page 87

Onion tart, recipe page 150

Chicken, leek and potato pie, recipe page 88

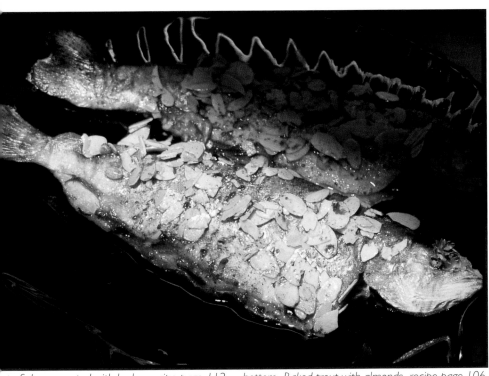

top Salmon crusted with herbs, recipe page 112　　*bottom* Baked trout with almonds, recipe page 106

Vegetable souffle, recipe page 51

Chocolate 'Bake it', recipe page 122

top Melting chocolate dessert, recipe page 129   *bottom* see Dessert recipes pages 117–134

Apple pie, recipe page 119

Buttery flavour 'Bake it', recipe page 122

Meat

Lamb Pork Beef

The Remoska is ideal for preparing meat dishes but in order to get the best results you need to follow some advice. If the meat needs browning first you will get a better result doing this in a frying pan and transferring it to the Remoska. Then continue with the recipe.

Turn the meat with two wooden spoons rather than a meat fork to avoid scratching the pan and also avoids the meat juices escaping by piercing.

Contents in this section

Irish Stew

Use the Grand Remoska – halve quantities for the Standard Remoska

50 g (2 oz) dripping
900 g (2 lb) stewing lamb
2 onions, peeled and sliced
500 ml (1 pt) chicken stock
1 bouquet garni (bay leaf, thyme, rosemary and parsley)

Salt and freshly ground black pepper

2 tbsp pearl barley
500 g (1 lb) potatoes, peeled and cut into chunks

1 tbsp chopped parsley

Heat dripping in a large frying pan and quickly fry the meat in small batches to brown on all sides. Remove the meat to the Remoska. Fry the onions in the remaining pan juice until lightly browned, add to the meat. Pour in the stock; add the bouquet garni and season. Sprinkle the barley over the meat. Cover and cook for one hour stirring occasionally. Add the potatoes and cook a further 30 minutes or until the meat is tender and potatoes are cooked.

Lamb Cutlets Wellington

4 best end neck of lamb cutlets

25 g (1 oz) butter

1 medium onion, peeled and finely chopped

175 g (6 oz) button mushrooms, finely chopped

Pinch of ground nutmeg

1 tbsp chopped parsley

Salt and freshly ground black pepper

100 g (4 oz) liver paté

2 tbsp double cream

225 g (8 oz) packet frozen puff pastry, thawed

1 egg, beaten

Sprigs of watercress

Trim excess fat from the cutlets and scrape the last 7.5 cm (3 in) of the bones clean with a sharp knife. Melt the butter in a frying pan and quickly brown the cutlets on both sides to seal in the juices. Remove from the pan and set aside to cool. Stir the onion and mushrooms into the pan juices and gently fry until they are cooked through and most of the liquid has evaporated. Remove the pan from the heat, stir in the nutmeg, parsley and season. Set aside to cool.

Beat the paté with the cream and spread this mixture over one side of the meat on the cutlets. Roll out the pastry thinly and cut it into four triangles. Divide the mushroom mixture equally and place in the centre of each triangle. Lay the lamb cutlets paté side down on top of the mushroom mixture. Fold the sides of the pastry triangle over the cutlets trimming off any excess pastry and leaving the scraped bone exposed like a small handle. Seal the parcel with beaten egg. At this point you may freeze the cutlets–open freeze for two hours, then pack in polythene bag.

Allow to thaw at room temperature for 1 ½–2 hours. Place in the Remoska, brush with a beaten egg and bake until pastry is well risen and golden brown, approx 30 minutes.

Garnish with watercress sprigs.

Lamb, Prune and Apple Casserole

4 lamb neck cutlets
2 tbsp oil
3 medium cooking apples
3 medium onions
6 ready to eat prunes
Salt and freshly ground
black pepper
150 ml (5 fl oz) brown stock
50 ml (2 fl oz) cider
1 tbsp of butter and 1 tbsp
of plain flour worked together
until smooth

Trim the cutlets, removing excess fat. Seal in hot oil. Peel, core and slice apples. Thinly slice the onions. Arrange half the apple and the onions in the bottom of the Remoska. Lay the lamb cutlets on top, season to taste. Add the prunes and a final layer of the remaining apples and onions. Pour over the stock and cider and cook for approx one hour. Whisk in the flour/butter mix and add more stock if needed. Cook for approx 30 minutes until the cutlets are tender and sauce thickened.

Roast Leg of Lamb stuffed with Plums
Use the Grand Remoska

2¹/2 kg (5 lb) leg of lamb
2 thick slices of white bread
50 ml (2 fl oz) port and a
little extra for the gravy
4 large red plums, stoned
3–4 sprigs of rosemary
25 g (1 oz) butter
425 ml (15 fl oz) stock
2 tbsp double cream
Salt and freshly ground
black pepper
Roasting bag

Ask your butcher to bone out the leg and trim off all excess fat. Soak bread in port and squeeze it out. Crumble bread and mix it with the sliced plums. Season and fill the cavity of the leg. Tie lightly with string to keep the shape. Make a few incisions on the surface of the lamb and insert little sprigs of rosemary.

Brush well with melted butter and place in a roasting bag or wrap in foil making sure the juices will not escape.

Place in the Remoska and roast for approx two hours. Carefully take out the roast to rest.

In a small saucepan reduce the stock, add to it the juices from the roast having first removed as much fat as possible, and bring to the boil. Add the extra port, double cream, and check for seasoning.

Sausage and Lamb Kidney Casserole

25 g (1 oz) butter or
margarine

225 g (8 oz) chipolata
sausages, halved

8 lambs' kidneys, skinned,
halved and cored

1 large onion, sliced

15 g (1/2 oz) plain flour

275 ml (10 fl oz) beef
stock (cube)

6 tbsp white wine

Salt and freshly ground
black pepper

1 tsp dried dill

100 g (4 oz) mushrooms,
sliced

700 g (1 1/2 lb) potatoes,
peeled, cooked and mashed

Beaten egg or melted butter
to glaze

Chopped parsley to garnish

Melt the fat in a frying pan and fry the sausages until they are lightly browned on all sides. Transfer them to the Remoska. Add kidneys to the frying pan and fry until well sealed. Add them to the Remoska. Cook the onion in the frying pan until softened. Stir in the flour, then add stock, wine, dill and seasoning. Bring to boil, stirring. Stir in the mushrooms and pour into the Remoska. Cover and cook for approx 30–40 minutes until the sausages and kidneys are tender.

Meanwhile, pipe the potato around the edge of a shallow flameproof serving dish. Brush the potato with beaten egg or melted butter and brown under a hot grill. Spoon the sausage and kidney casserole into the dish and garnish with parsley.

Spicy Lamb Chops

2 tbsp oil
4 lamb chump chops
1 Spanish onion, peeled
and sliced
1 green pepper, cored,
seeded and sliced
1 tsp ground cumin
1 tsp chilli powder
1 tbsp apricot jam
1 tsp tomato purée
1 tsp Worcestershire sauce
1 tbsp wine vinegar
275 ml (10 fl oz) chicken
stock
4 tomatoes, peeled, seeded
and chopped
50 g (2 oz) salted peanuts
Salt and freshly ground
black pepper
1 tbsp cornflour
2 tbsp water

Heat the oil in a large frying pan and quickly fry the chops on both sides, then remove them to the Remoska. Fry the onion and pepper in the pan juices until lightly browned. Add cumin and chilli powder to the onion and pepper and cook over high heat for two–three minutes, stirring constantly.

Lower the heat and add the apricot jam, tomato purée, Worcestershire sauce, vinegar, stock, tomatoes and peanuts to the pan and bring to boil. Season and pour over the chops.

Cover and cook for approx 40 minutes. Remove chops from the Remoska and arrange in a deep serving dish. Mix the cornflour with water and stir into the sauce. Replace the lid and cook until sauce is thickened approx ten minutes. Stir well and pour over the chops.

Serve with boiled rice.

Bacon and Sausage Bake

Butter for Remoska and
brushing top layer of potatoes
500 g (1 lb) potatoes,
peeled, cooked and sliced
4 rashers streaky bacon,
rinded and chopped
1 onion, finely chopped
225 g (8 oz) pork sausages,
skinned and quartered
2 eggs
150 ml (5 fl oz) milk
Salt and freshly ground
black pepper

Line the bottom of the buttered Remoska with half the potato slices. Mix together the bacon, onion and sausage pieces and place on top of the potato layer. Lightly beat the eggs with the milk, season and pour into the dish. Cover the top with the remaining potato slices, brush with butter. Bake approx 20 minutes.

Baked Pork Chops with Cream

4 pork chops
Salt and freshly ground
black pepper
1 large onion
700 g (1 1/2 lb) potatoes
4 slices of hard cheese, Edam
Emmenthal or similar
275 ml (10 fl oz) double
cream

Bone chops and with a wooden meat mallet
to tenderise, lightly season. Slice the onion and
spread on the base of the Remoska. Slice the
potatoes, layer over the onions and season.
Place chops on the sliced potatoes, top each
chop with a slice of cheese and pour over
cream. Bake approx 30–35 minutes. Serve
with a tomato and onion salad.

Variation – Replace cream with milk and a little
butter. To enhance flavour, top cheese slices
with crushed cloves of garlic.

Braised Pork Rolls with Mushrooms

2 tbsp vegetable oil
1 onion
1 large garlic clove
1 tsp caraway seed
200 g (7 oz) fresh
mushrooms
Salt and freshly ground
black pepper
1 egg, beaten
4 tbsp chopped parsley
4 pork steaks 125 g (5 oz)
each
150 ml (5 fl oz) chicken
stock

Heat one tablespoon of oil in the Remoska, add
finely chopped onion, chopped garlic, caraway
seed and fry until translucent. Add cleaned and
sliced mushrooms, season lightly and fry for a
further five minutes. Thicken with beaten egg
and stir in parsley. Leave to cool. Transfer to
a bowl. Clean Remoska.

With a wooden meat mallet flatten and lightly
season the pork steaks, place a spoonful of the
mushroom mixture at one end, roll up and
fasten the ends with a cocktail stick. Heat
remaining oil in the clean Remoska; add pork
rolls and brown on all sides. Add stock and
cook until tender, approx 30 minutes.

Serve with creamed potatoes and vegetables
of your choice.

Casseroled Pork with Caraway

500 g (1 lb) pork loin or
shoulder
3 garlic cloves, crushed
with 1 tsp salt
2 tbsp oil
1 tsp of caraway seed
150 ml (5 fl oz) stock
1 tbsp plain flour
75 ml (3 fl oz) water
Salt and freshly ground
black pepper

Rinse meat and cut into large cubes. Toss
with garlic crushed with salt. Heat the oil in
a frying pan, add the caraway seed and brown
the meat cubes on all sides. Transfer to the
Remoska. Add stock and continue to roast,
basting from time to time until tender, approx
40 minutes. Thicken the sauce with a paste
of flour and water, season and boil briefly.

Serve with potato dumpling and braised
white cabbage.

Curried Pork Loaf

350 g (12 oz) lean
minced pork
2 tsp curry powder
2 tbsp mango chutney
1 onion, finely chopped
50 g (2 oz) fresh breadcrumbs
Salt and freshly ground
black pepper
2 eggs, beaten
275 ml (10 fl oz) Béchamel
sauce (see page 137)
flavoured with curry powder

Mix together the pork, curry powder, chutney,
onion, breadcrumbs, season and bind with
the eggs. Press into a 500 g (1 lb) loaf tin and
smooth the surface. Place tin in Remoska (on a
circular mat of 'Magic Non-stick Liner' to avoid
scratching the pan). Pour warm water halfway
up the tin, close and bake for approx one hour.

Turn out onto a warmed serving dish and serve
with the 'curry' sauce. To serve cold–cool in the
tin and chill before turning out and slicing. Good
for a buffet, garnished with sweet-sour gherkins.

Pork and Apple Pie

1 pkt puff pastry rolled out thinly to fit circumference of the Remoska, prick all over with fork and leave to rest in the refrigerator

1 large onion, finely sliced
Grated rind of 1 lemon
1 pork loin thinly sliced– 10/12 slices
Salt and freshly ground black pepper
2 Cox's Apples, cored, sliced
275 ml (10 fl oz) white wine
275 ml (10 fl oz) water
50 g (2oz) butter
1 egg
150 ml (5 fl oz) double cream

Toss the sliced onion with the zest of the lemon and place a layer into the Remoska. Next a layer of pork slices on the onions, season and add a layer of sliced apples. Repeat the process and finish with a layer of sliced onions.

Mix wine with water, pour over the contents and dot with butter. Place the circle of puff pastry over the top, tucking the sides in, make a small cross in the centre and hold it open with a greased metal piping tube, brush with beaten egg. Cover with the lid and switch on, by the time the pastry is golden brown the pie should be cooked, approx 30 minutes. If you think the pastry is browning too fast, cover with a circle of foil or Magic Non-stick Liner.

When cooked, leave to stand for a few minutes, carefully remove the piping tube and pour in the warmed double cream. Leave for a few minutes. Serve directly from the pan.

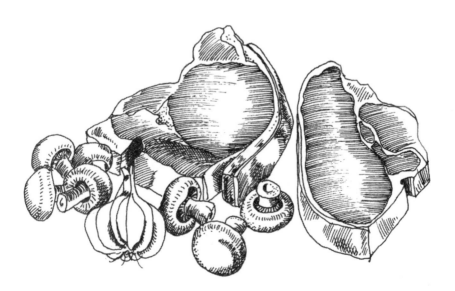

Pork and Garlic Sausage Casserole

3 tbsp oil

225 g (8 oz) lean rindless smoked bacon, diced

500 g (1 lb) lean shoulder of pork, trimmed and cut into 2.5 cm (1 in) cubes

1 large sliced onion

900 g (2 lb) potatoes, thickly sliced

275 ml (10 fl oz) light ale

Salt and freshly ground black pepper

225 g (8 oz) German garlic sausage

500 g (1 lb) sauerkraut, available in a Deli or supermarket, drained

2 red eating apples

1 tsp caraway seed

Heat oil in a frying pan and fry bacon for two–three minutes and lightly brown pork cubes. Remove with a slotted spoon onto a plate. Drain any fat from the frying pan into the Remoska and cook onion until soft.

Add meat and potatoes to Remoska stir in the ale, season, cover and cook for 45 minutes. Stir in the garlic sausage, drained and rinsed sauerkraut, sliced apples and caraway seed. Cook for a further 30 minutes or until the meat is tender.

Pork Chops and Mushroom Parcels

1 onion

2 garlic cloves

2 tbsp oil

200 g (7 oz) fresh mushrooms, sliced

1/2 tsp caraway seed

Salt and freshly ground black pepper

4 tbsp chopped parsley

2 tbsp double cream

4 pork fillets, 125 g (5 oz) each

Oil to coat foil

In a frying pan fry chopped onion and garlic in oil until translucent. Add sliced mushrooms, caraway seed, salt, and fry for a further three minutes. Stir in the chopped parsley and the double cream. Nick pork fillets around edges to prevent curling, lightly tenderise, (with a wooden meat mallet or a rolling pin) season lightly.

Place fillets on oiled aluminium foil squares, top with the cooked mushrooms and seal foil to keep juices from running out. Place packages in Remoska and bake approx 30 minutes until tender.

Serve with pan-fried or boiled potatoes.

Pork 'Cordon Bleu' with Apples

4 pork fillets, 225 g (8 oz) each

4 thin slices of boiled ham, to fit over half the fillet

4 thin slices of cheese, to fit over the ham–Gruyere

1 large Cox's apple, peeled and thinly sliced

Plain flour

2 eggs

Breadcrumbs to coat

Oil for shallow frying

Salt and freshly ground black pepper

Tenderise fillets (using a wooden meat mallet or a rolling pin), season lightly, top with ham and cheese slices and peeled apple slices. Fold fillets in half and pound edges together with a mallet, securing with a cocktail stick as needed. Dust on both sides with flour, dip in whisked eggs and coat with breadcrumbs. Heat oil in Remoska and fry the fillets on both sides until golden brown.

Serve with mashed potatoes and a fresh vegetable salad.

Milena's tip
The shallow Remoska pan is recommended for frying.

Roast Pork

500 g (1 lb) pork loin

1 tsp caraway seed

Salt and freshly ground black pepper

2 tbsp oil

Lightly salt the rinsed meat, sprinkle with caraway seed, heat oil in frying pan and brown on all sides. Transfer to the Remoska. Add a small amount of water to the pan and roast until tender, approx 40 minutes, occasionally basting with roasting juices. Serve with bread or potato dumplings, braised white cabbage or spinach.

Variation – Spread the surface of the pork loin with a mixture of one teaspoon of dry mustard mixed with two tablespoons of honey and roast as above.

Roast Pork larded with Carrot and Sausage

1 small carrot
1 Frankfurter sausage
500 g (1 lb) pork loin
3 garlic cloves, crushed with 1 tsp salt
Salt
1 tsp caraway seed
Pepper
1 onion
2 tbsp oil
150 ml (5 fl oz) chicken stock
1 tsp cornflour
50 ml (2 fl oz) water
Salt and freshly ground black pepper

Slice carrot and sausage into thin batons. Pierce rinsed pork loin with a sharp knife and insert carrot and sausage into the incisions. Lightly coat the meat with crushed garlic mixed with salt, sprinkle with caraway seed and pepper. Finely chop onion and fry lightly in oil in a frying pan, transfer to the Remoska, brown the meat on all sides in a hot frying pan and transfer to the Remoska.

Add stock and roast until tender, approx 40 minutes, occasionally basting with juices in the pan. When the meat is tender, remove to a warm place. Mix cornflour and water to a paste and stir into sauce in the pan to thicken. Cover and leave sauce to boil briefly.

Serve the roast sliced, with the sauce and boiled potatoes or rice and fresh vegetables.

Roast Pork with Cream Sauce

2 tbsp of oil
1 large onion
50 g (2 oz) celeriac, grated
1 carrot, grated
Salt and freshly ground black pepper
700 g (1 1/2 lb) pork loin
2 tbsp oil
150 ml (5 fl oz) chicken stock
1 tsp cornflour
150 ml (5 fl oz) double cream
50 g (2 oz) Cheddar cheese, grated
Pinch of grated nutmeg
4 tbsp chopped parsley or chives

Heat the oil in the Remoska, add finely chopped onion and cook until transparent, add grated celeriac and carrot, cover with lid, and cook for a further five minutes. Season the rinsed meat, brown on all sides in hot oil in a frying pan and place in the Remoska with the vegetables. Add stock, cover and roast until tender, approx 40 minutes, basting occasionally.

Remove meat to warm place. Add paste made of cornflour, cream, cheese, nutmeg and chopped chives or parsley to sauce. Cook until thickened.

Serve with rice or boiled potatoes and vegetables of your choice.

Stuffed Pork Fillet

2–3 pork fillets, 700 g (1 1/2 lb)
total weight
40 g (1 1/2 oz) butter
75 ml (3 fl oz) sherry,
or stock
1 tbsp plain flour
275 ml (10 fl oz) chicken
stock
Salt and freshly ground
black pepper

Stuffing
1 medium sized onion,
finely chopped
50 g (2 oz) butter
225 g (8 oz) minced veal,
or chicken
1 tbsp chopped parsley
1 tsp mixed herbs
1 tsp dried sage
Grated rind and juice of
1 lemon
4 tbsp fresh white breacrumbs
Salt and freshly ground
black pepper
1 egg

Split the fillets two thirds of the way through
and beat with a rolling pin or a meat tenderiser
to flatten.

Stuffing – In a frying pan cook onion in butter
until soft but not coloured. Add all other stuffing
ingredients and enough beaten egg to bind. Layer
stuffing between the fillets, shaping them to form
a loaf and tie up with string to keep the shape.

Heat the butter, add and then brown the pork
carefully on all sides. Transfer to the Remoska,
pour over the sherry or stock, close the lid and
cook for one hour or until pork is tender.

Take out the meat, sprinkle the flour onto the
pan juices, stir, replace lid and cook to thicken,
pour in the rest of the stock, stir, cover and cook
until boiling for two–three minutes. Remove the
string from the meat and serve sliced. Spoon a
little gravy round; serve the rest in a sauceboat.

Sweet and Sour Pork Balls

500 g (1 lb) lean minced pork
1 garlic clove, crushed
25 g (1 oz) fresh breadcrumbs
Salt and freshly ground
black pepper
1 tsp mixed dried herbs
1 egg beaten
Flour for coating
Oil for shallow frying
1 large red pepper, cored
seeded and sliced
200 g (7 oz) can crushed
pineapple
75 g (3 oz) brown sugar
4 tbsp cider vinegar
2 tbsp soy sauce
275 ml (10 fl oz) chicken
stock
1 tbsp cornflour

Mix together the pork, garlic, breadcrumbs, season, add herbs and bind with the egg. Shape into 16 balls and coat lightly with flour. In a frying pan shallow fry until golden brown on all sides. Drain well and place in Remoska.

Place red pepper, pineapple, sugar, vinegar, soy sauce and stock in a saucepan, season and bring to boil. Dissolve the cornflour with a teaspoon of water and add to pan. Stir and simmer until thickened. Pour sauce over the pork balls, cover and cook for approx 30–40 minutes.

Serve with boiled rice.

Beef Goulash

500 g (1 lb) braising steak
3 tbsp plain flour seasoned
with salt and freshly ground
black pepper
3 tbsp oil
500 g (1 lb) onions
6 large tomatoes
Salt and freshly ground
black pepper
250 ml (8 fl oz) beef stock
1 tsp sweet paprika
3 tbsp of sour cream, optional
but recommended

Cut the meat into cubes, toss in the flour and brown on all sides in two tablespoons of oil in a frying pan. Heat the remaining oil in the Remoska, finely slice the onion and cook until translucent, stirring occasionally. Add the meat, and scalded, peeled chopped tomatoes, season lightly, cover and cook until tender, (test the meat after 40 minutes) adding stock from time to time.

Immediately before removing goulash from pan, season with paprika and add the sour cream.

Serve with dumplings, boiled potatoes or bread.

Beef Goulash with Frozen Vegetables

2 large onions
1 tsp caraway seed
2 tbsp oil
500 g (1 lb) shin beef,
cubed
Salt and freshly ground
black pepper
275 ml (10 fl oz) tomato juice
500g (1 lb) frozen vegetables,
defrosted (mostly peppers
and tomatoes)

1 tsp sweet paprika
150 ml (5 fl oz) double cream
Juice of ½ lemon

In the Remoska fry finely chopped onion and caraway seed in oil until very pale gold, stir in cubed meat and brown on all sides. (You may like to do this part in a frying pan, if so now transfer to the Remoska.). Season to taste, add half the tomato juice and cook, stirring occasionally and basting with remaining tomato juice until the meat is tender, approx 40 minutes. Stir in frozen (defrosted) vegetables; sprinkle in the paprika and cook for a further five minutes. Stir in double cream and lemon juice. Adjust seasoning.

Serve with boiled potatoes, dumplings or bread.

Beef Goulash with Potatoes

500 g (1 lb) braising steak
3 tbsp plain flour seasoned
with salt and freshly ground
black pepper
3 tbsp oil
500 g (1 lb) onion
6 large tomatoes
425 ml (15 fl oz) beef stock
4 large potatoes, diced
1 tsp sweet paprika
1 slice of bread with
crust removed

Prepare the meat as in the previous recipe, Beef Goulash, page 77 and stew with onions and tomatoes and half the stock. After 45 minutes add peeled diced potatoes, cover with the remaining stock and simmer until the potatoes are cooked, approx 30 minutes. Season sauce with paprika, and thicken with crumbled bread.

Milena's tip
Thickening sauces with bread is a particular Czech custom – you may prefer to use cornflour and water

Beef 'Parcels' with Onions and Cheese

2 beef steaks 225 g (8 oz) each
1 tbsp olive oil
Salt and freshly ground black pepper
German mustard
1 onion
50 g (2 oz) Jarlsberg cheese, grated
2 heaped tbsp of tomato ketchup

Tenderise the steaks, nick edges, season lightly and brush with oil. Refrigerate for an hour. Place each steak on a piece of foil, lightly spread with German mustard, top with onion slices, season and seal to keep juices from escaping. Place the packages in the Remoska and bake until tender, approx 30 minutes. Carefully peel back foil, top with cheese, drizzle with ketchup and bake opened until the cheese has melted, approx ten minutes.

Serve with roasted potatoes or chips and salad.

Beef Steaks with Cream Sauce

4 beef steaks, 175 g (6oz) each
Salt and freshly ground black pepper
1 tsp ground sweet paprika
1 large onion
75 ml (3 fl oz) hot water
200 ml (7 fl oz) sour cream

Tenderise steaks and nick the edges on all sides, season, dust with paprika and place in Remoska. Sprinkle with chopped onion, add water and braise until tender, approx 20–30 minutes, basting occasionally. When meat is tender, remove from pan and thicken sauce with the sour cream. Return steaks to Remoska and warm through.

Serve with bread dumplings and green salad.

Beef Steaks with Peppers and Wine

*2 sirloin steaks,
225 g (8 oz) each*

1 tsp barbecue spice
2 tbsp mustard
2 tbsp olive oil for marinade
2 tbsp oil
1 onion, finely chopped
*2 medium sized peppers,
different colours if possible*

*Salt and freshly ground
black pepper*

150 ml (5 fl oz) red wine
150 ml (5 fl oz) water
4 tbsp chopped parsley

Tenderise the steaks until thin and nick the edges. Mix barbecue spice, mustard and oil, brush both sides of steaks and marinate for an hour in the refrigerator. Heat the oil in the Remoska, add the finely chopped onion and cook until transparent, add peppers cut into strips, season lightly and cook until tender. Remove from the pan; place the sirloin steaks in the same oil and brown on both sides. Add wine mixed with water and braise until tender, approx 30 minutes. Add the cooked vegetables for five minutes to reheat.

Place the steaks on plates, heap with onions and peppers, add the parsley to the sauce, mix and pour around.

Roast Fillet with cream sauce. 'Svíckovǎ'

Use the Grand Remoska

This is a classic Czech dish served at weddings, festivals, Sunday lunches and the pride of every restaurant. Dumplings are the Czech method but here you could use mashed potatoes.

Or why not taste it in Prague…

700 g (1 1/2 lb) fillet of beef
50 g (2 oz) smoked bacon in one thick slice
200 g (7 oz) mixed root vegetables, carrot, celeriac, parsnip)
1 onion
2 tbsp oil
Grated rind of 1 lemon
5 black peppercorns
3 bay leaves
1 tsp dried thyme
Pinch of allspice
6 tbsp water
1 tbsp plain flour
3 tbsp water
275 ml (10 fl oz) soured cream
Juice of 1/2 lemon
Salt and freshly ground black pepper

Remove any membranes from the meat, cut bacon into strips about the thickness of a pencil and making incisions in the meat, 'lard' it with the bacon. Finely slice the root vegetables and the onion. Heat oil in a frying pan, add the onion, and cook until soft, add the sliced root vegetables, and fry for a few minutes. Transfer to the Remoska. In the frying pan brown the meat on all sides and place in the Remoska. Add the grated lemon rind, peppercorns, the bay leaves, thyme, allspice and the six tablespoons of water. Cover and roast approx 40–45 minutes or until tender, occasionally basting it with the juices.

Remove the meat and keep warm. Mix the flour with three tablespoons of water to make a paste, add to the pan juices, stir and cover to boil and thicken. Tip all the gravy with the cooked root vegetables into a liquidiser, whiz up, add the sour cream, and lemon juice, whiz once more, season to taste and return to the Remoska.

The sauce should have a slightly sour taste but very fingerlicking. Reheat the sauce to serve with slices of the meat, the dumplings, a slice of lemon and cranberries.

No vegetable is served with this dish. It's one of those dishes where "his mother always made the best 'Svícková' in the world….!"

Risotto with Sausage

2 tbsp oil
1 onion
2 garlic cloves
225 g (8 oz) sausage,
a good ham salami or
French garlic sausage

Pinch of saffron
4 large ripe tomatoes
Salt and freshly ground
black pepper

350 g (12 oz) Risotto rice
500 ml (1 pt) ham
stock (cube)

Pinch of chilli pepper,
optional

4 tbsp chopped parsley
Freshly grated Parmesan

Fry chopped onion and finely chopped garlic
in oil in the Remoska until translucent, stir in
salami or garlic sausage cut into small cubes,
saffron, scalded, peeled, deseeded and chopped
tomatoes, season, cover and cook for six–eight
minutes. Add rinsed rice and stir until it soaks
up residual liquid. Pour in warm stock, stir,
cover and cook until rice is tender and the
stock absorbed, approx 20 minutes. Stir
chopped parsley and pinch of chilli pepper
into cooked risotto.

Serve with freshly grated Parmesan.

Poultry and Game

When roasting poultry, game or rabbit, it is better to have it portioned.
Small chicken may be roasted whole, but do take into account
that they will take longer than portioned chicken.

Contents in this section

Chicken Breasts Fried with Bacon and Peppers

4 boned chicken breasts
Salt and freshly ground
black pepper
1 tbsp oil
100g (4 oz) smoked bacon
1 onion
2 large peppers of different
colours
2 tbsp tomato purée
1 tsp dried marjoram
4 large potatoes, peeled
and cubed
400 ml (14 fl oz) chicken
stock
1 tbsp of plain flour
3 tbsp water
2 tbsp freshly chopped
parsley

Tenderise chicken breasts lightly, season and brown on both sides in hot oil in the Remoska. Remove and keep warm. Cube the bacon, add to the pan and leave to brown. Add the chopped onion, the peppers cut into strips and fry briefly. Stir in tomato purée, marjoram, potatoes, add the stock, season to taste and leave to cook. When potatoes are almost tender, return the chicken breasts to the Remoska and continue cooking.

When potatoes and meat are tender, approx 30 minutes, remove the chicken breasts and thicken sauce with a tablespoon of flour mixed with water, add parsley and simmer until the sauce thickens.

Chicken Breasts with Cheese Sauce and Mushrooms

4 boned chicken breasts
Salt and freshly ground
black pepper
2-3 tbsp oil
1 onion, finely chopped
225 g (8 oz) mushrooms
100 ml (4 fl oz) chicken stock
100 g (4 oz) Cheddar cheese,
grated
4 tbsp chopped parsley or
chives
Pinch of grated nutmeg
Few drops of Worcestershire
sauce

Tenderise chicken breasts; season lightly and brown on both sides in hot oil in a frying pan. Remove and add the onion, cook to soften, add sliced mushrooms and fry briefly. Place the onion/mushroom mix into the Remoska, add chicken breasts, stock and roast until tender and golden brown, approx 30 minutes. Remove meat from pan, add grated cheese, parsley or chives, flavour with nutmeg and Worcestershire sauce.

Serve with sauce poured over the chicken, with boiled or fried potatoes and a green salad.

Chicken Breasts with Peaches

4 boned chicken breasts
3 tbsp of oil
Salt and freshly ground
black pepper
2 garlic cloves
1 tsp of dried marjoram
2 fresh peaches
4 slices of cheese,
Emmenthal
1 tsp sweet paprika

Tenderise chicken breasts and brush with one tablespoon of oil seasoned with salt and freshly ground black pepper, crushed garlic and the marjoram. Refrigerate for one hour.

In a frying pan brown the breasts on both sides in the remaining oil and transfer to the Remoska. Peel and slice peaches, place on the chicken breasts, top with cheese slices, sprinkle lightly with paprika and cook in the Remoska until the cheese starts to melt.

Serve with roasted potatoes or chips and salad.

Chicken Drumsticks in Wholegrain Mustard, Olive Oil and Herbs

2 tbsp wholegrain mustard
2 tbsp olive oil
1 heaped tbsp mixed dry
Herbs of Provence
8 chicken drumsticks

In a bowl mix together the mustard, oil and the herbs. Stir the drumsticks in the mix coating them well, cover with cling film and leave in the refrigerator for at least one hour or overnight. Place drumsticks in the Remoska and roast until golden brown, approx 30–40 minutes. Excellent for picnics. If the drumsticks make too much juice, pour most of it off half way (approx 20 minutes) and cook until crisp and golden brown.

Chicken Fried with Vegetables

2 peppers of different colours
1 courgette
1 onion
1 chicken, 1 ½ kg (2–2½ lb)
portioned
3 garlic cloves crushed
with 1 tsp salt
Oil for shallow frying
4 large tomatoes, peeled
and chopped
250 ml (8 fl oz) chicken stock
175 ml (6 fl oz) double cream
1 tbsp plain flour
1 tbsp dried marjoram
4 tbsp chopped parsley
Salt and freshly ground
black pepper

Cut washed and cleaned peppers into strips, slice the courgette and finely chop the onion. Rub chicken portions with garlic crushed with salt and fry in hot oil in the Remoska together with vegetables and onion until the chicken pieces are pale gold. Stir in tomatoes, add the stock and simmer until tender. When the chicken pieces are tender, approx 45 minutes, remove from pan and keep warm. Mix together the cream and flour and add to the pan juices. Stir in marjoram, chopped parsley and simmer briefly until sauce thickens. Season to taste.

Serve the meat and sauce with boiled potatoes or rice.

Chicken Mandarin

Cornflour for coating
Salt and freshly ground
black pepper
4 chicken joints, skinned
2 tbsp oil
225 g (8 oz) tin of
mandarin oranges
275 ml (10 fl oz) Béchamel
sauce (see page 137)
½ tsp dried tarragon
2 tbsp Cointreau or other
orange liqueur
75 g (3 oz) unsalted peanuts,
chopped

Mix the cornflour with salt and pepper and use to coat the chicken joints. Heat the oil in a frying pan and brown the chicken joints on all sides. Transfer them to the Remoska. Drain the mandarin oranges and add the syrup to the Béchamel sauce with the tarragon and Cointreau. Pour the sauce over the chicken, cover and cook approx 30–40 minutes or until the chicken is tender. Add the mandarin oranges and sprinkle the peanuts on top. Cook for a further five minutes.

Chicken Parcels with Horseradish

4 boned chicken breasts
German mustard
Salt and freshly ground
black pepper
Oil to brush on foil
4 rashers of bacon
2 large tomatoes
I good tbsp of freshly grated
horseradish, if you are unable
to find fresh horseradish use
from a jar

Lightly tenderise chicken breasts, brush with
mustard and season. Place each chicken breast
on a square of foil, top with bacon, tomato slices
and horseradish. Seal foil in order to keep juice
from escaping, place in the Remoska and bake
until tender, approx 45 minutes but check after
30 minutes.

Serve with roast potatoes or chips and
mixed salad.

Chicken, Leek and Potato Pie

2 large chicken breasts
I large carrot
I celery stick
I bay leaf
Fresh sprigs of thyme
Slice of onion or leek top
250 ml (8 fl oz) Béchamel
sauce (see page 137)
100 ml (4 fl oz) chicken stock
2 medium leeks, washed and
sliced into 2 cm (I in) pieces
I red and I green pepper,
seeded and diced
I tbsp chopped fresh parsley
or dill

Topping
500 g (I lb) potatoes
50 g (2 oz) butter
100 ml (4 fl oz) single cream
or milk
Salt and freshly ground
black pepper

Poach chicken breasts in water to cover with the
carrot, celery, bay leaf, thyme and onion or leek
top, simmering for approx 15 minutes. Leave to
cool in stock.

Make your Béchamel sauce and add stock.
Season well. Blanch the leek pieces and the
peppers, drain well. Take all the meat from the
chicken breasts and cut into cubes. Fold this,
the drained vegetables and the parsley or dill
into the Béchamel sauce. Spoon the mixture
into the base of the greased Remoska. The
dish may be prepared to this point, cooled
and refrigerated.

Peel potatoes, cut into even-sized pieces and
cook in salted water. Drain and mash with the
butter and cream or milk. Season and spoon
smoothly over the chicken. Cover with lid and
cook until topping is golden brown and bubbling,
approx 30 minutes.

Curried Chicken Drumsticks and Thighs

4 chicken thighs and
4 drumsticks
1 tsp minced chilli pepper
1 tsp curry paste
Salt
2 tbsp oil
2 onions, finely chopped
225 g (8 oz) ripe tomatoes,
scalded, peeled and chopped
200 ml (7 fl oz) chicken stock
4 tbsp chopped parsley or
chives

Brush chicken with mixture of minced chilli pepper, curry paste and salt and brown in hot oil in the Remoska. Remove chicken and keep warm, add the onion to the remaining oil and cook until translucent. Return chicken to pan. Add tomatoes, pour over half the stock and cook until chicken is tender and the sauce thickens, approx 30 minutes, adding stock as needed. Finally stir in the parsley or chives.

Serve with boiled potatoes or rice and green salad.

Poultry 'Burgers' Chicken or Turkey

2 thick slices of granary bread
150 ml (5 fl oz) milk
350 g (12 oz) cooked turkey
or chicken
2 eggs
2 heaped tbsp Cheddar
cheese, mature, grated
2 tbsp chopped parsley
Salt and freshly ground
black pepper
Breadcrumbs for coating
Oil for shallow frying

Soak crumbled bread in milk. Squeeze out excess milk. Meanwhile mince the chicken or grind in a food processor. Stir in eggs, cheese, parsley, soaked bread, season and mix thoroughly. Form mixture into small 'burgers', coat with breadcrumbs and place in hot oil in the Remoska. Fry on both sides and place on paper towel to drain off excess oil.

Serve with mashed potatoes, mayonnaise or ketchup and green salad.

Roast Chicken

1 chicken, quartered
1 tsp barbecue spice
4 tbsp oil
Oil to coat pan
Salt and freshly ground
black pepper

Coat chicken in oil mixed with barbecue spice and place in the oiled Remoska. Roast approx 45 minutes depending on the size of the chicken. If too much juice comes from the bird pour some off halfway through the cooking. This will result in a lovely crisp chicken.

Variation – Instead of barbecue spice, use oil mixed with garlic crushed with salt and a pinch of ground sweet paprika. Or use oil mixed with fresh herbs such as rosemary or thyme. If you wish, place thickly sliced potatoes, onions and parsnips under the chicken pieces. They will absorb the juices and be delicious.

Roast Chicken with Almond Stuffing

Stuffing
2 whole-wheat bread rolls
cut into cubes
100ml (4 fl oz) milk
100g (4 oz) butter
2 eggs, separated
Grated rind of 1 lemon
Pinch of grated nutmeg
4 tbsp chopped parsley
Salt and freshly ground
black pepper
100g (4 oz) ground almonds

1 chicken, 1 1/2 kg (2–2 1/2 lb)
3 tbsp oil

Prepare stuffing. Soak bread in milk, beat butter until soft, stir in egg yolks, add soaked bread, lemon rind, nutmeg, parsley and season. Fold in almonds and stiffly whisked egg whites.

Stuff the rinsed, seasoned chicken, heat oil in the Remoska, brush the chicken with a little hot oil. Place the chicken in hot oil and roast until tender, golden brown and crispy, approx 50–60 minutes or until juices run clear.

Serve with potatoes prepared according to preference and fresh salad or vegetables of your choice.

Roast Lemon Poussin

2 Poussins (baby chickens)
around 400 g (14 oz)
2 tbsp lemon juice
Salt and freshly ground
black pepper
2 garlic cloves
1 preserved or fresh lemon,
quartered
Handful of basil leaves
1 tbsp butter
1 extra lemon, quartered

Clean poussins and wipe dry. Rub each poussin with lemon juice, then with salt and black pepper. Slip garlic cloves, preserved or fresh lemon quarters and basil leaves in cavity of each bird. Roast poussins in Remoska, basting occasionally with melted butter and lemon juice until thigh juices run clear when pierced with a skewer, approx 40 minutes.

Allow to cool to room temperature then cut each bird in two using a heavy knife, cutting down one side of the back-bone.

Serve with extra lemon quarter for squeezing.

Spanish Style Chicken

4 tbsp olive oil
4 chicken pieces, thighs
and breast
1 large onion, sliced
2 garlic cloves, crushed
1 green and 1 red pepper,
sliced
1 small tin of chopped
tomatoes
Large pinch of saffron
1 tbsp sweet paprika
350 g (12 oz) Risotto rice
Salt and freshly ground
black pepper
150 ml (5 fl oz) dry white wine
425 ml (15 fl oz) chicken
stock
Small amount of chopped
parsley

Heat oil in a large frying pan and brown chicken pieces. Transfer to the Remoska. Add onions, peppers, garlic and tomatoes to the frying pan and cook for a further five minutes.

Transfer to the Remoska together with the saffron, paprika, rice, the seasoning, then wine and stock. Cook for approx 30–40 minutes until all liquid is absorbed and the rice is cooked.

Serve sprinkled with a little chopped parsley.

Spicy Roast Chicken

4 portions of chicken
1 tsp German mustard
4 tbsp soy sauce
4 tbsp oil
1 tsp barbecue spice
Black pepper to taste

Mix together the mustard, soy sauce, oil, barbecue spice, freshly ground black pepper and brush chicken portions with the marinade. Refrigerate at least six hours or overnight.

Do not salt the meat, as the soy sauce and barbecue spice are salty enough. Place the chicken portions in the Remoska and roast until golden and tender, approx 30 minutes, basting occasionally with the seasoned oil. If too much juice appears, pour some of it off half way through the cooking (approx 15 minutes). This will make the chicken crisp.

Serve with potatoes prepared according to preference and fresh salad or vegetables of your choice.

Variation – While the chicken is roasting, add peeled, parboiled sliced potatoes tucked around and roast together until tender.

Baked Turkey Breasts with Apples

2 slices of turkey breast,
175 g (6 oz) each
Salt and freshly ground
black pepper
3 tbsp oil
2 thin slices of ham
1 apple
2 thin slices of cheese,
Emmenthal
1 tsp sweet paprika

Lightly tenderise turkey breast, season and fry on both sides in hot oil in a frying pan. Layer each piece of meat with a ham slice, peeled, cored and sliced apple and a slice of cheese sprinkled with paprika. Place in the lightly oiled Remoska. Bake until cheese starts to melt, approx 20 minutes.

Serve with your choice of potatoes and fresh salad.

Roast Stuffed Turkey Breast

*2 thick slices of turkey breast
300 g (10 oz) each*
*Salt and freshly ground
black pepper*
Flour for dusting
100 ml (4 fl oz) white wine
100 ml (4 fl oz) chicken stock
3 tbsp oil
*2–3 slices of Turkey ham for
'repairs'*
Stuffing, see page 90

Prepare stuffing as in the recipe for 'Roast Chicken with Almond', see page 90. If there is some left over, bake it separately. Cut turkey breasts along one side in order to make a pocket. Tenderise lightly in order to make pocket larger for stuffing. If the meat tears, patch with a slice of turkey ham to keep stuffing from running out. Stuff breasts and fasten opening with a cocktail stick. Season lightly, dust with flour; place in heated oil in the Remoska and brown on both sides. Add white wine, cover and when it cooks off add stock and cook until meat is tender, approx 20 minutes, turning once or twice. Serve with boiled potatoes and vegetable salad or cooked vegetables of your choice.

Turkey Roulades with Ham and Spinach

1 small onion
1 garlic clove
*100 g (4 oz) frozen spinach,
defrosted*
*100 g (4 oz) of ham or ham
salami*
*50 g (2 oz) Cheddar or Edam,
cheese, grated*
4 slices of turkey breast
*Salt and freshly ground
black pepper*
Oil as needed
100 ml (4 fl oz) white wine
100 ml (4 fl oz) water

In a frying pan fry finely chopped onion and garlic in a tablespoon of oil until translucent, add the defrosted and squeezed out spinach, season and fry for a further five minutes. Leave to cool and stir in the finely cubed ham and grated cheese.

Tenderise turkey breasts, season lightly and spread spinach mixture on top, leaving at least 1 cm (½ in) from edge free to keep filling from escaping during cooking. Roll up breasts, fasten the end with a cocktail stick, place in heated oil in the Remoska and brown on all sides. Baste with wine mixed with the same amount of water and continue cooking until tender, approx 20 minutes.

Serve with boiled or mashed potatoes.

Duck Breast Chinese Style with Pineapple

*2 duck breasts, 225 g (8 oz)
each*
Salt
1 tbsp plain flour
2 tbsp oil
1 tbsp grated fresh ginger
1 leek, chopped
1 onion, chopped
2 carrots, chopped
1 tbsp soy sauce
1 tbsp brown sugar
2 tbsp tomato purée
2 tbsp dry vermouth
100 ml (4 fl oz) white wine
100 ml (4 fl oz) water
¹/2 tsp cornflour
3 tbsp water
*2 slices tinned pineapple,
cut into cubes*
*Salt and freshly ground
black pepper*

With a sharp knife score the skin side of the duck breast diagonally across in a large diamond pattern. Season with salt, dust lightly with flour and in a pre-heated frying pan fry on both sides in hot oil. Start with the skin side and fry until crisp, turn over and seal the other side. Remove to a warm place. Pour off some of the duck fat. In remaining pan juices fry the ginger, add leeks, onion and carrots. Fry the vegetables for three minutes. Place everything in the Remoska, add soy sauce, brown sugar, tomato purée, vermouth and the duck breasts. Baste with wine and water, cover and cook meat and vegetables until tender, approx 30 minutes. Remove breasts again. Stir in cornflour mixed with three tablespoons of water, pineapple, return breasts to pan and heat through.

Serve with rice.

Variation – Substitute chicken pieces or turkey breast for duck.

Pheasant with Apple

1 pheasant
*Salt and freshly ground
black pepper*
100 g (4 oz) butter
*500 g (1 lb) eating apples,
peeled, cored and thinly
sliced*
4–5 tbsp single cream

Rub the pheasant with salt and pepper. Melt the butter in a frying pan and brown the pheasant on all sides. Put half the apples in the Remoska and pour over a little of the butter from the pan. Place the pheasant in the Remoska and cover with rest of the apples. Pour over remaining butter from the pan and the cream. Cover and cook for approx 30 minutes or until the pheasant is tender.

Pheasant with Apples and Cream

1 large pheasant	In a pan brown the pheasant all over in half the
75 g (3 oz) butter	butter. Set aside. Peel, core and slice the apples;
4 medium sized Russets or	fry lightly in the rest of the butter, sprinkling them
Cox's Apples	with cinnamon as they cook. Place a layer of
1 tsp cinnamon	apples in the Remoska, lay the pheasant on
100 ml (4 fl oz) double cream	top breast down and tuck the rest of the apples
Salt and freshly ground	round the sides. Pour in half the cream, cover
black pepper	and cook for approx one hour. After 30 minutes
2 tbsp Calvados	turn the bird breast side up, seasoning it with

1 large pheasant
75 g (3 oz) butter
4 medium sized Russets or Cox's Apples
1 tsp cinnamon
100 ml (4 fl oz) double cream
Salt and freshly ground black pepper
2 tbsp Calvados

In a pan brown the pheasant all over in half the butter. Set aside. Peel, core and slice the apples; fry lightly in the rest of the butter, sprinkling them with cinnamon as they cook. Place a layer of apples in the Remoska, lay the pheasant on top breast down and tuck the rest of the apples round the sides. Pour in half the cream, cover and cook for approx one hour. After 30 minutes turn the bird breast side up, seasoning it with salt and pepper and continue roasting until the pheasant is golden brown and tender, approx 40 minutes.

Remove the pheasant, stir in the rest of the cream and the Calvados.

Carve the pheasant and place on a bed of apple and cream sauce on a serving dish. Chicken may be cooked in the same way.

Rabbit Braised with Onions

1 rabbit
100 g (4 oz) thick slice of smoked bacon cut into larding strips
Salt and freshly ground black pepper
1–2 tsp dried thyme
2 tbsp oil
2 large onions
250 ml (8 fl oz) chicken stock

Cut cleaned rabbit into portions, lard with bacon, season, sprinkle with thyme and in a frying pan brown in oil. Remove rabbit and place in the Remoska. Add finely chopped onion to oil in the pan and fry until translucent. Transfer to the rabbit portions, add stock, cover and cook until tender, approx 40 minutes.

Serve with boiled potatoes and compote of cranberries.

Rabbit Parcels

500 g (1 lb) boned rabbit
meat
Salt and freshly ground
black pepper
Sprig of fresh or
1 tsp dried rosemary
2 tbsp lemon juice
1 carrot, washed and grated
2 sticks of celery, finely
chopped
1 large parsnip, peeled
and sliced
4 tbsp chopped parsley
1 large onion, finely chopped
4 tbsp ketchup
Dash of Worcestershire sauce
Oil for foil

Slice rabbit meat, preferably from loin, into strips, season, toss with rosemary, drizzle with lemon juice and leave briefly in a cool place.

Mix rabbit meat with the carrot, celery, parsnip and parsley. Divide mixture into four equal portions. Place each portion in oiled foil, sprinkle with onion, drizzle with ketchup and Worcestershire sauce. Seal edges of foil thoroughly to lock in juices, place in the Remoska, cover and bake until tender, approx 40 minutes.

Serve with potatoes prepared according to preference and salad.

Roast Rabbit with Vegetables and Mushrooms

1 rabbit, portioned
Salt and freshly ground
black pepper
2 tbsp oil
1 large onion
2 garlic cloves
250 ml (8 fl oz) chicken
stock
100 g (4 oz) fresh
mushrooms, sliced
2 carrots, finely chopped
2 leeks, finely chopped
4 tbsp chopped parsley
250 ml (8 fl oz) double cream

Season the cleaned and portioned rabbit and in a frying pan brown on both sides in hot oil. Place in the Remoska. Add finely chopped onion and chopped garlic to fat in pan. When onion turns golden, add to the rabbit in the Remoska. Add stock, cover and cook until almost tender, approx 40 minutes. Add mushrooms, vegetables, cook another ten minutes. Stir in parsley, cream and cook for five more minutes.

Serve with dumplings or boiled potatoes.

Roast Rabbit with Mushrooms

1 rabbit
Salt and freshly ground
black pepper
2 tbsp oil
250 ml (8 fl oz) chicken stock
2 large garlic cloves, crushed
225 g (8 oz) mushrooms
4 large tomatoes, scalded,
peeled and chopped
4 tbsp chopped parsley

Cut cleaned rabbit into portions, season and in a frying pan brown on both sides in hot oil. Place in the Remoska, add stock, cover and roast until tender, approx 40 minutes. Add garlic, cleaned and sliced mushrooms, tomatoes and cook for a further ten minutes. Stir in a four tablespoons chopped parsley.

Serve with boiled potatoes and a mixed salad.

Roast Rabbit with Tomatoes

1 rabbit
Salt and freshly ground
black pepper
2 tbsp vegetable oil
2 large onions, finely chopped
500 g (1 lb) ripe tomatoes
150 ml (5 fl oz) chicken stock

Cut the cleaned rabbit into portions, season. In a frying pan fry the rabbit portions until light brown on both sides. Remove meat from pan, add onion to the remaining oil in pan and cook until translucent. Place in the Remoska, add the rabbit pieces, scalded, peeled and chopped tomatoes, the stock and roast until tender, approx 45 minutes.

Serve with boiled potatoes.

Venison Family Casserole
Use the Grand Remoska – halve quantities for the Standard Remoska

Basic marinade
4 tbsp olive oil
2 tbsp red wine or dry sherry
(wine vinegar as a last resort)
1 tsp grated lemon rind
1/2 tsp freshly grated nutmeg
1 tbsp crushed juniper berries
1/2 garlic clove, crushed
Salt and freshly ground
black pepper

Combine all the ingredients of the basic marinade in a screw top jar and shake well. It will keep in the refrigerator for three weeks.

In a large pan stir-fry the vegetables in a little oil. Add garlic, marinated venison and bacon stirring well. Add the flour, stock and wine and stir again. Transfer to the Remoska, cover and cook for approx 1–1 1/2 hours until the meat is tender.

2 tbsp oil
100 g (4 oz) button
mushrooms
1 large sliced onion
1 green pepper, sliced
4 carrots, sliced
2 celery sticks, chopped
1/2 clove garlic, crushed
1 kg (2 lb) casserole venison
in cubes, marinade overnight
in basic marinade

100 g (4 oz) diced gammon
or bacon
25 g (1 oz) plain flour
275 ml (10 fl oz) chicken
stock
75 ml (3 fl oz) of red wine

Venison in Foil

500 g (1 lb) haunch of
venison
Salt and freshly ground
black pepper
4 thin rashers of streaky
bacon
1 large onion
4 tbsp chopped parsley
4 tbsp white wine
4 tbsp natural yoghurt or
sour cream
4 tbsp ketchup

Cut cleaned haunch into four slices, tenderise
well and season. Place venison slices on foil,
top with bacon slices, sliced onion and parsley,
drizzle with white wine and top with sour
cream or yoghurt mixed with ketchup. Seal
foil thoroughly to lock in juices and bake in the
Remoska until tender, approx 30–40 minutes.

Serve with baked potatoes or French fries and
salad. If you have a 'Grand' Remoska the baked
potatoes will sit on top of the foil parcels.

Venison Ragout with Mushrooms

500 g (1 lb) haunch of
venison
Salt and freshly ground
black pepper
2-3 tbsp oil
3 large onions
225 g (8 oz) mushrooms
100 ml (4 fl oz) white wine
350 g (12 oz) tomatoes
200 ml (7 fl oz) beef stock
250 ml (8 fl oz) sour cream
1 tsp plain flour
4 tbsp chopped parsley

Cut the venison meat into cubes, season and
in a frying pan brown on all sides in hot oil.
Transfer to the Remoska. Fry finely chopped
onion in the same oil until translucent, add
cleaned, sliced mushrooms, and fry until they
start releasing juices. Add to the meat in the
Remoska, add wine, cover and cook until
the wine has reduced. Add scalded, peeled,
chopped tomatoes, the stock and cook
until tender, approx 40 minutes.

Mix the sour cream with flour, add to
the pan, stir in parsley and cook briefly
until sauce thickens.

Serve with dumplings, rice or pasta.

Braised Roulades of Venison

500 g (1 lb) haunch of venison

Salt and freshly ground black pepper

4 garlic cloves

Mustard, 1 tsp for each slice

4 rashers of bacon

1 large onion

2–3 tbsp oil

250 ml (8 fl oz) chicken stock

Cut cleaned haunch into four slices, tenderise well, season, rub with crushed garlic, spread with mustard, top with bacon slices and finely sliced onion. Roll up each slice of meat; fasten with string or cocktail stick and in a frying pan brown on all sides in hot oil.

Transfer to the Remoska. Add stock and braise until tender, approx 40–50 minutes.

Serve with boiled potatoes or rice and salad.

Fish

Fish is at its best when it is fresh.

When buying fish look for,
1 *fish free from any strong odour*
2 *red gills*
3 *bright eyes*
4 *firm flesh*
5 *a stiff tail, a flabby tail is a sure sign that fish is not fresh.*

Contents in this section

Baked Cod with Caraway Seed

500 g (1 lb) cod steaks
Juice of 1 lemon
Salt and freshly ground
black pepper
50 g (2 oz) butter
2 tsp caraway seed

Drizzle cleaned fish portions with lemon juice, season lightly, place in hot melted butter in the Remoska with the caraway seed and brown on both sides, approx seven minutes each side.

Serve garnished with chopped parsley or chives and parboiled fried potatoes.

Baked Cod with Garlic

500 g (1 lb) cod steaks
Juice of 1 lemon
3 large garlic cloves,
crushed with 1 tsp salt
Plain flour for dusting
1/2 tsp sweet paprika
Butter for Remoska
4 tbsp chopped parsley
or chives
Salt and freshly ground
black pepper

Drizzle cleaned fish portions with lemon juice, rub with crushed garlic, dust with flour mixed with half teaspoon of sweet paprika, place in buttered Remoska and bake until golden brown, approx 20 minutes.

Sprinkle baked fish portions with chopped parsley or chives, season and serve with potatoes. Fish portions may be topped with herb or melted butter.

Baked Fish Roulades

500 g (1 lb) white fish fillets
Juice of 1 lemon
1 onion
1 tsp ginger
8 large leaves of Chinese or
regular cabbage
1 egg
100 ml (4 fl oz) double cream
2 tbsp Gruyere cheese,
grated
Pinch of grated nutmeg
Oil for pan
Salt and freshly ground
black pepper

Lightly poach fish fillets in salted water with lemon juice, cool and blend in a food processor together with the onion and the ginger. Rinse and briefly cook in a small amount of simmering water (just to soften) the cabbage leaves. Then lay carefully on a clean tea towel and pat dry. Divide fish mixture into eight portions and place on the cabbage leaves. Roll up and place in the lightly greased Remoska.

Whisk up the egg with cream, cheese and nutmeg, pour over the fish roulades and bake until the top browns, approx 20 minutes.

Baked Mackerel

2 mackerel, gutted and
scales removed

1 tsp finely chopped fresh
sage leaves

1 garlic clove, crushed

1 cm (¹/2 in) fresh root ginger,
grated or minced

2 tsp lemon juice

2 tbsp olive oil

1 thin rasher of streaky
bacon, rind removed,
finely chopped

1 large tomato

Salt and freshly ground
black pepper

Make three diagonal cuts on each side of the
fish. Place in the Remoska. Mix sage, garlic,
ginger and lemon juice with olive oil, pour over
the fish and season. Leave in a cool place to
marinate for an hour. Baste occasionally.

Mince the bacon or whiz in a food processor.
Scald and skin the tomato, cut out core, remove
seeds and chop roughly. Press a little of the
bacon into the cuts in the fish, cover with
chopped tomato and spoon over the marinade.
Cover with lid and bake approx 20 minutes.
Arrange the fish on a serving dish and
keep warm.

Transfer the tomatoes and all the juices in the
Remoska to a smaller saucepan, bring to boil
and boil hard for a few minutes to reduce the
sauce. Pour over the fish and serve at once.

Baked Mussels with Leeks

500 g (1 lb) leeks

25 g (1 oz) butter

1 tbsp oil

225 g (8 oz) frozen shelled
mussels

100 g (4 oz) frozen peas

250 ml (8 fl oz) Béchamel
sauce (see page 137)

50 g (2 oz) Swiss or other
cheese, grated

3 tbsp chopped parsley

2 tbsp lemon juice

Salt and freshly ground
black pepper

Slice rinsed leeks into rings and place in the
Remoska with butter and a tablespoon of oil.
Add partially thawed mussels and frozen peas
and stir. Pour on Béchamel sauce mixed with
Swiss cheese and half of the parsley. If needed,
add extra seasoning and lemon juice. Bake
approx 30 minutes or until the top begins
to brown.

Sprinkle with the rest of the parsley. Serve
with potatoes or freshly baked bread rolls.

Baked Plaice with Orange Juice

500 g (1 lb) plaice fillets
Salt and freshly ground
black pepper
Oil for Remoska
6 small tomatoes, scalded
and peeled
Juice of 1 large orange
100ml (4 fl oz) white wine
Pinch of saffron
2 tbsp fresh breadcrumbs
25g (1 oz) butter

Lightly season plaice and put in oiled Remoska.

In another bowl mix tomatoes cut into chunks with orange juice, wine, saffron, pinch of salt and spoon over fish. Sprinkle with breadcrumbs, dot with butter and bake for approx 20–25 minutes.

Serve with potatoes and fresh vegetables.

Baked Salmon with Mustard Sauce

500 g (1 lb) piece of salmon
Salt and freshly ground
black pepper
1 large onion
2 large garlic cloves
50 g (2 oz) butter
Mustard sauce, see page 139
Parsley, chopped

Place lightly seasoned salmon in the oiled Remoska. Sprinkle with finely chopped onion and garlic, dot with butter and bake for approx 15–20 minutes. Meanwhile, prepare mustard sauce, spoon over baked salmon to serve.

Serve with boiled potatoes sprinkled with chopped parsley.

Baked Trout with Almonds

2 small trout
Juice of I lemon
Salt and freshly ground
black pepper
Seasoned plain flour
for coating
2 tbsp oil
50 g (2 oz) sliced almonds
2 tbsp butter
I lemon
2 tbsp parsley or chives,
chopped

Drizzle trout with lemon juice and season. Dust with seasoned flour and place in a small amount of hot oil in the Remoska. Cook on both sides.

Meanwhile dry fry the almonds in a frying pan until lightly brown. Place trout on plate, top with brown butter, (melt in a small frying pan and heat until it turns light brown, taking care not to burn it), sprinkle the trout with almonds, and garnish with lemon pieces, chopped parsley or chives.

Serve with potatoes, and a selection of vegetables of your choice.

Baked Whiting with French Mustard Sauce

Butter for Remoska
2 whiting, cleaned and filleted
Salt and freshly ground
black pepper
2 tbsp onion or spring onion,
finely chopped
4 tbsp dry white wine or cider
I tbsp French mustard
I tbsp grated lemon rind
Juice of 1/2 lemon
I tbsp chopped parsley
25 g (I oz) butter
2 tbsp double cream (optional)
Chopped parsley to garnish

Lay the fillets in the buttered Remoska. Season and sprinkle with chopped onion or spring onion. Mix together wine or cider, mustard, lemon rind and juice and pour over the fish. Cover and bake for approx 20 minutes or until tender.

Strain the cooking liquor into a saucepan and simmer for approx two–three minutes. Stir in the parsley, butter and cream if used, heat through gently.

Arrange fish fillets on a warmed serving plate and pour over sauce. Garnish with parsley.

Devilled Cod

Butter for Remoska
2 cod cutlets, 225 g (8 oz)
each
15 g (¹/2 oz) butter
Salt and freshly ground
black pepper

'Devil'
1 tbsp Worcestershire sauce
6 tbsp tomato ketchup
Pinch of cayenne pepper
1 tsp anchovy essence
Dash of Tabasco sauce
Garnish with sprigs of parsley

Arrange cutlets in the buttered Remoska.
Dot with butter and season. Cover and bake
for approx 20 minutes or until the fish will
flake easily.

Meanwhile, put all the ingredients for the 'devil'
in a saucepan and heat through, stirring.

Transfer the fish to a warmed serving dish and
pour over the 'devil'. Garnish with parsley.

Fillet of Fish baked with Tomatoes

4 fillets, 225 g (8 oz) each
choice of plaice, hake, or
halibut
Juice of 1 lemon
Salt and freshly ground
black pepper
1 tsp of sweet paprika
4 tomatoes
1 tsp dried thyme or
other mixed herbs
2 tbsp olive oil

Drizzle fillets with lemon juice, season lightly,
sprinkle with paprika, (this is best done through
a very fine sieve) and place in the oiled Remoska.
Rinse tomatoes, cut X on the top, season, add
thyme or mixed herbs, drizzle with olive oil and
place with the fish in the Remoska. Cook for
approx 25 minutes.

The tomatoes may be prepared this way
separately and served as an accompaniment
to other fish, meat or poultry.

Fish and Spring Greens Pie

*225 g (8 oz) white fish cod,
haddock or whiting*

100 g (4 oz) uncooked prawns

100 g (4 oz) prepared scallops

100 g (4 oz) smoked haddock

*225 g (8 oz) spring greens or
Savoy cabbage, coarsely
chopped*

*500 g (1 lb) potatoes, peeled
and cut into equal pieces*

50 g (2 oz) butter

100 ml (4 fl oz) milk

*500 ml (1 pt) Béchamel sauce
(see page 137)*

100 g (4 oz) Cheddar, grated

*1 leek, washed and very finely
shredded*

*Salt and freshly ground
black pepper*

25 g (1 oz) butter

Dry the fish and seafood thoroughly with kitchen paper and cut into bite size pieces. Arrange the spring greens in the base of the Remoska, cover with fish and seafood.

Cook potatoes in boiling, salted water for approx 20 minutes or until tender. Drain, return to the saucepan and mash well adding butter, milk and season to taste. Beat well and set aside until needed.

Make Béchamel sauce and add the grated cheese. Pour over fish. Sprinkle the finely chopped leek over the top. Spoon the mashed potato evenly over the leek and run a fork over the surface for a traditional look. Dot with the 25 g (1 oz) of butter, put the lid on and bake for approx 20 minutes or until the surface is golden brown. If browning too quickly cover the potatoes with a circle of foil.

Fish au Gratin

*500 g (1lb) white fish fillets
cod, hake, halibut*

*300 g (10 oz) canned
condensed mushroom soup*

2 tomatoes, sliced

*50 g (2 oz) cheese, your
choice, grated*

Toast triangles to garnish

Arrange the fish fillets in the Remoska. Heat soup and pour over fish. Cover and bake for 15 minutes. Uncover, top with tomato slices and grated cheese. Replace lid and bake for further five minutes or until the cheese has melted.

Garnish with toast triangles.

Fish Cakes

500 g (1 lb) poached fish,
cod, haddock or salmon
2 medium potatoes
2 tbsp chopped parsley
1 whole-wheat roll moistened
in 100 ml (4 fl oz) milk
4 tbsp Jarlsberg cheese,
or similar, grated
1 egg
Salt and freshly ground
black pepper
Breadcrumbs for coating
Oil for shallow frying

Mince or finely flake fish. Boil potatoes in their jackets, peel, mash with fork, and stir in the fish, add chopped parsley, the squeezed out roll, grated cheese, the beaten egg, season to taste and mix thoroughly. Form into round fish cakes and coat in breadcrumbs. Fry on both sides in hot oil in the Remoska until golden brown.

Serve with mashed potatoes and ketchup or tartare sauce.

Fish Cakes coated with Corn Flakes

500 g (1 lb) any kind of boned
fish, hake, cod, haddock
400 g (14 oz) potatoes
50 g (2 oz) butter
2 eggs
2 tbsp chopped parsley
Salt and freshly ground
black pepper
Plain flour
100 g (4 oz) crushed
corn flakes
Oil for shallow frying

Mince the raw fish or poach and mash with fork. Boil potatoes in their jackets in lightly salted water, peel whilst still hot and mash, adding butter.

Mix fish with cooled mashed potatoes, one egg, parsley, and season to taste. If the mixture is too thin, thicken with breadcrumbs. Form into fish cakes, dust with flour, dip in beaten egg and coat with crushed corn flakes. Place cakes in heated oil in the Remoska and fry on both sides until golden brown.

Serve with creamed potatoes.

Fish Kebabs

Best in the shallow pan of the 'Grand' Remoska

*500 g (1 lb) frozen white
fish steak
1 lemon
Salt and freshly ground
black pepper
1 green pepper
1 onion
1 small courgette
2 large firm tomatoes
225 g (8 oz) mushroom caps
1 tsp barbecue spice for fish
2 tbsp oil
Oil for shallow frying*

Cut partially thawed fish into 2 cm (1 in) cubes drizzle with lemon juice and lightly season. Do not thaw fillets completely to keep from falling apart when threading on the skewers. Alternate with chunks of pepper, onion wedges, courgette, tomatoes and cleaned mushroom caps. Mix oil with barbecue spice and pinch of pepper. Heat the oil in the Remoska. Place skewers in pan and baste occasionally with oil mixture. Cook for approx 20 minutes.

Serve with potatoes and green salad or a selection of vegetables of your choice.

Fish Risotto

*2 tbsp olive oil
1 onion
500 g (1 lb) boned fish, cod,
hake, halibut, smoked haddock
300 g (10 oz) tomatoes
100 g (4 oz) tin of sweetcorn
1 bay leaf
1 tsp ground ginger
Pinch of saffron
Salt and freshly ground
black pepper
300 g (10 oz) Risotto rice
500 ml (1 pt) fish stock
(cube) more if necessary
4 tbsp chopped parsley
Generous quantity of
grated Parmesan*

Fry finely chopped onion in oil in the Remoska, add fish cut into serving pieces, stir to coat them in oil, add scalded, peeled, chopped tomatoes, sweetcorn, bay leaf, ginger and a pinch of saffron. Season, add rinsed rice and stir well. Add warm stock, cover and cook until rice has absorbed all the stock, approx 30 minutes. More stock may be needed depending on the rice. When ready, remove bay leaf and stir in chopped parsley.

Serve with grated Parmesan.

Fried Plaice with Ham

4 fillets of plaice 225 g (8 oz) each

Juice of I lemon

Salt and freshly ground black pepper

4 thin slices of boiled ham

Plain flour

I egg

4 tbsp fresh breadcrumbs

50 g (2 oz) grated cheese

Oil for shallow frying

Drizzle plaice with lemon juice, lightly season and roll up in ham slices. Coat with flour, beaten egg and the breadcrumbs mixed with cheese. Heat oil in the Remoska. Fry on all sides until golden brown. Serve with lemon wedges, potatoes and tartare sauce.

Gratin of Prawns with Potatoes

500 g (I lb) potatoes

I garlic clove, cut in half

40 g (I ¹/2) oz butter

250 ml (8 fl oz) beef stock

225 g (8 oz) cooked peeled prawns

100 ml (4 fl oz) double cream

Salt and freshly ground black pepper

Pinch of nutmeg

I tsp fresh dill

50 g (2 oz) Gruyere cheese, grated

Peel and thinly slice potatoes. Rub garlic around the inside of Remoska and then brush with melted butter. Place potatoes in Remoska, season, pour over the stock, cover with lid and cook for 30 minutes. Add prawns.

Mix the cream with salt, pepper, nutmeg, the dill and pour over the potatoes and prawns. Bake for another 15 minutes. Sprinkle with grated cheese, dot with remaining butter, cover once more and cook for a further five minutes to melt the cheese.

Halibut Bake

Butter for Remoska

2 halibut steaks 225 g (8 oz) each

150 ml (5 fl oz) dry cider

Large pinch of ground mace

I tsp fresh herbs, parsley, thyme, rosemary and tarragon, finely chopped

Arrange halibut steaks in the buttered Remoska. Mix together cider, mace and herbs and pour over the fish. Cover and bake for approx 15–20 minutes or until fish will flake easily.

'Jarlsberg' Cod

Butter for Remoska
500 g (1 lb) fillet of cod
1 tsp salt
1/2 tsp white pepper
1 garlic clove, crushed
2 medium tomatoes, peeled
and sliced
1 small leek, thinly sliced
225 g (8 oz) Jarlsberg cheese,
grated
100 ml (4 fl oz) single
cream or milk

Place serving size pieces of cod into the buttered Remoska. Season with salt, pepper and garlic. Arrange tomato slices and leek over the fish. Top with cheese and pour cream or milk over. Bake for approx 20 minutes or until fish flakes and the cheese is golden brown.

Salmon crusted with Herbs

4 salmon steaks, 175 g (6 oz)
each
Salt and freshly ground
black pepper
100 g (4 oz) butter
Mixture of herbs, 1 heaped
tsp of each dried parsley,
dill, basil, tarragon and
fennel seed
1 thick slice of white bread

Season and brush salmon fillets with melted butter. Take all the herbs and the slice of bread and whiz them in a food processor to obtain rough crumbs. Spread evenly over the salmon. Drizzle the rest of the butter over the top, place in the Remoska and cook for approx 25 minutes. The salmon should be moist and flaky and the crust golden brown.

Serve with creamed potatoes, spinach and a side tomato salad.

Salmon with Watercress Cream

Butter
Salt and freshly ground
black pepper
4 salmon cutlets to fit in
the Remoska
4 bay leaves

Cut four squares of foil large enough to enclose a salmon cutlet. Butter foil and sprinkle with salt and pepper. Place a cutlet on each square and dot with more butter, place a bay leaf on top. Wrap foil around the cutlet and bake for 15 minutes or until cooked through. Cool in foil packets.

Watercress cream
1 bunch of watercress
150 ml (5 fl oz) double cream
Salt and freshly ground
black pepper
1 tbsp lemon juice

Simmer watercress in boiling water until tender. Drain well and blend to a purée. Mix with remaining ingredients and chill. Remove salmon cutlets from foil and discard cooking juices and bay leaves. Arrange cutlets on a serving plate and serve with the watercress cream.

Seafood Bread and Butter Pudding

10 slices from a small
sandwich loaf
Meat from a large crab or
300 g (10 oz) shelled prawns
Salt and freshly ground
black pepper
Cayenne pepper
Tender celery stalk,
finely chopped
1 tbsp chopped onion
150 ml (5 fl oz) mayonnaise
3 tbsp mixed fresh herbs–
parsley, tarragon, chervil and
chives, chopped
3 tbsp Parmesan cheese,
grated
100 g (4 oz) Gruyere or
Gouda cheese, grated
4 eggs
150 ml (5 fl oz) milk
250 ml (8 fl oz) single cream

Butter the bread and cut off crusts. Season the crab or prawns. Mix celery, chopped onion and mayonnaise, herbs and Parmesan and then fold in the shellfish. Make five sandwiches with the mixture.

Butter the Remoska. Cut sandwiches in half diagonally and place, overlapping, in the Remoska. Dot with the grated Gruyere or Gouda. Beat the eggs with the milk and cream and pour through a sieve over the sandwiches in the pan. Leave in the fridge two hours or longer (could be overnight).

Bake until top is crispy and brown, approx 30 minutes.

Seafood Risotto

2 tbsp olive oil
1 onion
2 garlic cloves
225 g (8 oz) frozen seafood,
defrosted
100 ml (4 fl oz) white wine
4 large ripe tomatoes
Salt and freshly ground
black pepper
350 g (12 oz) Risotto rice
500 ml (1 pt) vegetable stock
4 tbsp chopped parsley
Parmesan cheese, grated

Fry chopped onion and garlic in oil in the
Remoska, add seafood, cook briefly for five
minutes, add wine, scalded, peeled, chopped
tomatoes, season and cook for a further ten
minutes. Stir well-rinsed rice into the Remoska,
add stock and cook for a further 20–30 minutes
or until stock is absorbed.

Serve sprinkled with chopped parsley. Grated
cheese optional.

Seared Salmon with Sweet Peppers

1 tbsp olive oil
4 salmon fillets, 225 g (8 oz)
each
1 tbsp olive oil
1 tsp sweet paprika
Salt and freshly ground
black pepper
2 roasted red peppers
1 tsp olive oil
Bunch of watercress
2 tbsp olive oil for the dressing
1 tbsp lemon juice or red
wine vinegar
1 tsp caster sugar
1 tbsp small capers

Heat one tablespoon olive oil in the Remoska.
Trim salmon fillets removing any pin-bones with
tweezers. Mix a tablespoon of olive oil, paprika,
seasoning and coat the salmon with the spiced
oil. Leave in a cool place for 15 minutes. Place
salmon skin side down in the Remoska and bake
for 10–15 minutes. Meanwhile skin the roasted
peppers; cut flesh into fine strips and coat in
a little extra olive oil. Rinse the watercress, shake
dry and pick off the leaves, discard the stems.

Make the dressing by whisking the olive oil,
lemon juice or vinegar, sugar, salt and freshly
ground black pepper in a bowl until lightly
thickened. Toss the watercress in this dressing
and arrange on four dinner plates. Place salmon
fillets on top and arrange peppers and capers
on top of each fillet.

Shark Steaks with Herb Butter

500 g (1 lb) shark steaks or
other firm fish such as tuna
Juice of 1 lemon
1 tsp barbecue spice for fish
Plain flour
2 tbsp oil
Herb butter
Salt and freshly ground
black pepper

Drizzle shark steaks with lemon juice, dust with barbecue spice and leave to marinate for an hour. Dust steaks with flour and fry on both sides in the Remoska until golden brown, brushing occasionally with oil. Remove the skin from the shark before serving topped with herb butter.

Smoked Fish Pie

Butter for Remoska
500 g (1 lb) smoked haddock
fillet (frozen–but defrosted
is an alternative)

500 g (1 lb) new potatoes
100 g (4 oz) button
mushrooms
40 g (1 1/2 oz) butter
25 g (1 oz) plain flour
450 ml (16 fl oz) milk
100 g (4 oz) frozen peas
Salt and freshly ground
black pepper
25 g (1 oz) melted butter

Poach the fish in the milk for approx 15–20 minutes until it will flake easily. Strain off the milk and keep for the sauce. Add to fresh milk to make up the quantity in the recipe.

Scrub the potatoes but do not peel; cook in boiling salted water and drain and peel. Wipe and slice the mushrooms. Melt the butter in a saucepan, add the mushrooms and cook for a few minutes. Take the pan off the heat and stir in the flour. Add the milk and stir the sauce until simmering. Add the peas and simmer for approx three minutes. Flake the fish and stir into the mixture. Season to taste.

Spoon the mixture into the Remoska, cut the potatoes in half lengthways placing them cut side up over the top. Brush the surface with melted butter, cover and bake to a pale gold, approx ten minutes.

Serve with fresh tomato salad.

Milena's tip
Fish is at its best when it is fresh.

When buying fish look for,
1 *fish free from any strong odour*
2 *red gills*
3 *bright eyes*
4 *firm flesh*
5 *a stiff tail, a flabby tail is a sure sign*
   that fish is not fresh.

When removing the skin of fish, put a small
amount of salt on the ends of your fingers,
this provides a better grip.

Desserts

When baking, instead of buttering and flouring the pan, we strongly recommend the 'Magic Non-stick Liner Circles Ref 3325[*] and the baking parchment Cake Tin Liners Ref 5551[*], neither of which need to be buttered or floured. You may put the cake mixture directly onto the Magic Non-stick Liner or in the Cake Tin Liner.

It is easier to take pastry out of the Remoska using the liner and there is no danger of the pastry breaking up.

You may use the Magic Liner in the Remoska for any kind of cooking. Use the Magic Non-stick Liner on the base of your oven to keep it clean. It is virtually indestructible and it just wipes clean.

[*]available from Lakeland Limited

Contents in this section

Apple Pie

100 g (4 oz) unsalted butter
125 g (5 oz) caster sugar
3 eggs, separated
125 g (5 oz) self-raising flour
Unsalted butter and plain
flour for Remoska
500 g (1 lb) eating apples
1 tsp of cinnamon mixed
with 3 tsp caster sugar
Vanilla sugar

Cream softened butter with sugar and whisked egg yolks. Stir in sifted flour and finally fold in stiffly beaten egg whites. Pour batter into buttered and floured Remoska lined with baking parchment or 'Magic Non-stick Liner' and top with peeled, sliced apples. Sprinkle with cinnamon and sugar mix and bake until golden, approx 35–40 minutes. Sprinkle cooled pie with vanilla sugar.

Not your everyday Apple Pie

Unsalted butter and flour
for Remoska
75 g (3 oz) unsalted butter
75 g (3 oz) icing sugar
1 egg
1/2 tsp crushed cloves
1/2 tsp ground cinnamon
Grated rind of 1 lemon
2 tbsp cocoa
225 g (8 oz) self raising flour
50 ml (2 fl oz) milk

Topping
350 g (12 oz) peeled and
grated eating apples
25 g (1 oz) caster sugar
50 g (2 oz) raisins soaked in
2 tbsp of rum for 15 minutes
50g (2 oz) walnuts,
roughly chopped

Butter and flour the Remoska. Cream softened butter, sugar and egg, cloves, cinnamon and lemon rind. Add sifted cocoa powder with the flour, add milk and stir into a 'slack' mix. Pour this into the Remoska lined with baking parchment or 'Magic Non-Stick Liner' and spread evenly with a spatula. Cover batter with apples tossed in the caster sugar, sprinkle with raisins and walnuts and bake approx 35–40 minutes.

Apple and Marzipan Puffs

500 g (1 lb) block fresh or
defrosted puff pastry
300 g (10 oz) marzipan
3 tbsp lemon curd
2 dessert apples, Cox's or
Braeburn, cored, quartered
and sliced
1 tbsp milk
3 tbsp apricot glaze,
warmed through

Heat 3 tbsp apricot jam,
passed through a sieve
onto a saucer

Roll out pastry 3 mm ($^1/_4$ in) on a floured
surface, prick all over and using an 8 cm (3 in)
plain cutter cut out 8 circles. Place 4 circles in
the Remoska. Roll out the marzipan and using
a 6 cm (2 in) cutter cut out 8 circles of marzipan.
Place 1 on each circle of pastry and spread over
1 tsp of lemon curd. Arrange the apple slices
over the lemon curd. Brush the edges of the
pastry with milk, cover and bake for approx
15–20 minutes. Allow to cool before lightly
brushing with warm apricot glaze. Repeat
with 4 pastry circles.

Serve with lightly whipped cream.

Milena's tip
The 'Grand' Remoska will take all
8 Apple and Marzipan Puffs at one go.

Apple Bread and Butter Pudding

8 large slices of white bread
100 g (4 oz) unsalted butter
4 dessert apples
100 g (4 oz) caster sugar
Pinch of ground cinnamon
40 g (1 $^1/_2$ oz) raisins soaked
in dark rum
500 ml (1 pt) milk
2 eggs

Cut bread slices diagonally across into triangles,
brush both sides with melted butter and place
half in the base of the buttered Remoska. Peel,
core and slice the apples, toss with half the
sugar, cinnamon and pre-soaked raisins, lay
them on the bread slices, cover with the
rest of the bread.

Whisk up eggs with milk and pour through
a sieve over prepared pudding, leaving it for
ten minutes to absorb the liquid before baking.
Drizzle with any leftover melted butter, bake
to golden crispy brown, approx 40 minutes.

Sprinkle with the rest of the sugar whilst
still warm.

Austrian Coffee Cake

175 g (6 oz) unsalted butter
175 g (6 oz) caster sugar
3 eggs
175 g (6 oz) self-raising flour
Pinch of salt
250 ml (8 fl oz) strong black coffee
Sugar and rum or brandy to taste
250 ml (8 fl oz) double cream
1–2 drops vanilla extract
1 tbsp of browned, flaked almonds
Ring mould 750 ml (1 1/2 pt) capacity

Cream butter and sugar until light and fluffy. Beat in the eggs a little at a time; lastly fold in sifted flour with a pinch of salt. Turn the mixture into the greased ring mould, place in the Remoska and bake for approx 25–30 minutes. Test with a wooden cocktail stick. When baked, turn out and set aside to cool.

Clean the ring mould and when the cake is cold place back in the ring mould. Sweeten the coffee to taste and flavour with rum or brandy. Pour slowly over the cake while in the mould and leave for a while for the liquid to soak in.

Turn out for serving, coat with whipped cream mixed with vanilla extract and scatter with flaked almonds.

Bake it! – The Easiest Cake in the World

Next time you are shopping in your local Sainsbury supermarket look for a Nestlé® product called 'Bake It'.

Bake it – Buttery or Chocolate flavour

This cake mix could have been invented for the Remoska. You will find it on the chilled shelf of your Sainsbury supermarket.

Line your Remoska with a Lakeland Cake Tin Liner. Just cut open the corner of the packet of Bake It and squeeze the ready mixed contents straight into the paper case. Cover and switch the lid on. After 20 minutes cover the top of the cake with a circle of foil with the centre cut out, the Remoska cooks slightly quicker round the edge than in the centre. Bake for another five minutes, cover the whole cake with Magic Non-Stick Liner Circle, switch off and leave the cake to cool in the Remoska.

If you are using the Buttery flavour then I suggest you make a lemon or orange drizzle, dilute sieved icing sugar with enough juice of a large lemon or orange to make a runny sauce and pour it on the cake whilst still warm, it's a real winner.

The chocolate cake responds wonderfully to being covered with melted chocolate sauce. First spread the cake with a light coat of warm seedless raspberry jam and when that has cooled off float the melted chocolate over the top – your very own Sachertorte…

Milena's tip
You can be really clever, use half buttery and half chocolate mix and make a marble cake, with the remaining halves make individual fairy cakes.

Melt 225 g (8 oz) quality plain chocolate, when smooth but not too hot stir in 25 g (1 oz) unsalted butter, take care not to get the butter 'oily'. Pour all of it onto the chocolate cake, tip the cake from side to side to distribute the sauce evenly and leave it to run down the side. You should have a beautifully smooth surface. Smooth the side with a spatula.

Baked Apples with Lemon and Vanilla Sauce

500 g (1 lb) dessert apples,
Cox's, Russet or Braeburn
75 g (3 oz) any type of jam
50 g (2 oz) ground walnuts
50 g (2 oz) unsalted butter
Unsalted butter for Remoska

Vanilla Sauce
500 ml (1 pt) milk (or half
double cream, half milk)
3 egg yolks
1 tsp vanilla sugar
2 heaped tbsp caster sugar
1 heaped tbsp sifted
plain flour
1 tbsp lemon juice
Grated lemon rind

Core and peel apples, fill with jam mixed
with ground walnuts, brush with melted butter.
Place in buttered Remoska and bake approx
30 minutes.

Meanwhile, combine milk, egg yolks, vanilla
and caster sugar, plain flour and a drop of lemon
juice in a pan, slowly bring to simmering point
and boil, stirring constantly until sauce thickens.
Remove from heat and continue stirring until
sauce cools down, then whisk in a tablespoon
of lemon zest and the lemon juice. Do not
add lemon zest and juice to hot sauce, or it
will curdle.

When serving pour the sauce around the
baked apples.

Milenas tip
Bramleys are not suitable for this recipe.

Baked Bananas

Unsalted butter for Remoska
4 large bananas, peeled and
halved lengthways
25 g (1 oz) unsalted butter
50 g (2 oz) brown sugar
Grated rind and juice of
1 orange
Grated rind and juice of
1 lemon
2–3 tbsp rum

Arrange bananas in the buttered Remoska, dot
with unsalted butter and sprinkle with the sugar,
orange and lemon rinds. Mix together fruit juices
and rum and pour over the top. Close the lid
and bake for 15–20 minutes. Serve hot or cold.

Baked Dessert with Forest Fruit

4 egg yolks
100 g (4 oz) caster sugar
100 ml (4 fl oz) white wine
Unsalted butter for Remoska
500 g (1 lb) fruit (strawberries, raspberries, blueberries,
blackberries)
Vanilla sugar for topping

Beat together egg yolks and sugar until creamy and add wine. Place bowl over a pan with barely simmering water and whisk until the content doubles in volume. The water in the pan must not boil otherwise the yolks will curdle. Pour sauce into buttered Remoska, cover with fruit, sprinkle with vanilla sugar and bake until golden, approx 15–20 minutes.

Baked Noodles with Cream Cheese

300 g (10 oz) broad noodles
40 g (1 1/2 oz) unsalted butter
225 g (8 oz) soft cream
cheese, Quark or Ricotta
3 eggs
75 g (3 oz) caster sugar
Grated rind from 1 lemon
100 g (4 oz) raisins, soaked
in dark rum (15 minutes)
100 ml (4 fl oz) milk
Unsalted butter for Remoska
Salt

Pasta makes very good 'sweet puddings'.

Boil noodles according to instructions in lightly salted water, drain and toss with butter. Mix cream cheese with one egg, half of the sugar, grated lemon rind, and raisins. Spread half of the noodles in the buttered Remoska, top with cream cheese mixture and cover with remaining noodles. Cover with lid and bake, approx 15–20 minutes. When noodles are almost baked, pour the other two eggs whisked with milk over the top and bake until crisp and golden brown, approx ten minutes. Whilst warm, sprinkle with remaining sugar.

Baked Noodles with Fruit

350 g (12 oz) broad noodles
Salt
40 g (1 1/2 oz) unsalted butter
Unsalted butter for Remoska
225 g (8 oz) fruit in season
(apricots, cherries, plums, etc)
100 g (4 oz) ground walnuts
75 g (3 oz) caster sugar
2 eggs
100 ml (4 fl oz) milk
Unsalted butter for Remoska

Boil noodles in lightly salted water, drain and toss with butter. Spread half of the noodles in the base of buttered Remoska, top with a layer of cut up, pitted fruit, sprinkle with ground walnuts, half of the sugar and cover with remaining noodles. Cover with Remoska lid and bake for approx 20 minutes. When noodles are almost done, pour eggs beaten with milk over top and finish baking until crisp and golden brown, approx ten minutes. Sprinkle warm dessert with remaining sugar.

Baked Pancakes

Pancakes
100 g (4 oz) plain flour
275 ml (10 fl oz) milk
Pinch of salt
4 eggs
50 g (2 oz) unsalted butter
Extra butter for frying and
buttering the Remoska

Filling
350 g (12 oz) cheese,
Quark or Ricotta
50 g (2 oz) caster sugar
(more if you like the
filling sweeter)

2 egg yolks
1 tsp lemon rind, grated
1 tsp vanilla sugar
Pinch of salt

To bake
250 ml (8 oz) single cream
2 eggs
50 g (2 oz) icing sugar

With the pancake mix make 8 pancakes. For the filling, blend the cheese with sugar, egg yolks, lemon rind and vanilla sugar. Put a spoonful of this filling on each pancake and roll up, starting at one end, tucking the round edges over the filling and rolling on to make a neat parcel. Place in the buttered Remoska. Whisk up the single cream, the eggs and icing sugar, pour over the pancakes and bake for approx 15–20 minutes until the sauce has set. Serve hot sprinkled with icing sugar.

Blueberry Pie

225 g (8 oz) plain flour
75 g (3 oz) caster sugar
100 g (4 oz) unsalted butter
2 egg yolks
1 tsp vanilla sugar
Pinch of salt
1 egg white
225 g (8 oz) blueberries or
blueberry jam, no sugar
needed
50 g (2 oz) caster sugar,
mixed with 1 tsp of cinnamon

Make pastry with flour, sugar, butter, beaten egg yolks, vanilla sugar and a pinch of salt. Wrap in foil and refrigerate for an hour. Divide dough into two, one part slightly larger. Using the larger, roll out a 5 mm (¼ in) thick circle and transfer to Remoska or line a flan tin that will fit into the Remoska. Prick all over for an even bake. Roll out remaining dough and cut in to 1 cm (½ in) strips. Toss blueberries with cinnamon sugar and spoon onto the pastry or use blueberry jam. Use the pastry strips to make a grid over the fruit, press down well on edges, brush with beaten egg white, cover and bake until golden, approx 30 minutes.

Variation – Use strawberries, pitted and sliced, apricots, plums or peaches.

Carrot Soufflé

100 g (4 oz) icing sugar
4 eggs, separated
125 g (5 oz) carrots, peeled
and finely grated
100 g (4 oz) ground almonds
75 g (3 oz) dried breadcrumbs
2 tbsp dark rum
Unsalted butter and breadcrumbs for coating pan

Sauce
100 g (4 oz) apricot jam
4 tbsp hot water

Cream sugar with yolks and stir in finely grated carrot, ground almonds, breadcrumbs, rum and fold in stiffly beaten egg whites. Pour batter into buttered and breadcrumb-coated Remoska and bake until risen and golden, approx 40 minutes.

Make sauce by thinning the jam with hot water.

Carefully turn out the baked soufflé onto a platter, sieve hot apricot sauce over soufflé and chill until it sets.

Cheese and Cranberry Scones

225 g (8 oz) self-raising flour
I tsp baking powder
Pinch of salt
50 g (2 oz) unsalted butter
75 g (3 oz) Stilton or Danish Blue cheese, crumbled
100 ml (4 fl oz) milk
40 g (1 1/2 oz) dried cranberries
I egg beaten

Sift the flour and baking powder into a bowl, add salt. Rub in butter with fingertips; add most of the cheese, reserving a small amount for top of the scones. Add milk and the cranberries and mix well together to form soft dough. Turn out onto a floured board, roll out to 2 cm (1 in) thickness and cut into 5 cm (2 in) rounds.

Place in the Remoska lined with Magic Non-Stick Liner or baking parchment, brush tops with a little beaten egg and sprinkle with the rest of the cheese. Bake for 10–12 minutes until risen and light golden brown.

Cheesecake

I tsp baking powder
225 g (8 oz) plain flour
125 g (5 oz) unsalted butter
75 g (3 oz) icing sugar
I egg
Grated rind of I lemon
Unsalted butter and plain flour for coating Remoska

Filling
500 g (1 lb) soft cream cheese, Quark or Ricotta
100 g (4 oz) icing sugar
I egg
2 tbsp custard powder
100 g (4 oz) raisins, soaked in rum
50 ml (2 fl oz) milk
75 ml (3 fl oz) vegetable oil
100 g (4 oz) very finely chopped almonds, hazelnuts, or walnuts for topping

Make pastry with the sifted baking powder and flour, butter, sugar, egg, and lemon rind, (best made in a food processor). Roll out into thin circle and with the help of a rolling pin transfer to buttered and floured, or lined with Magic Non-Stick Liner, Remoska leaving the edges raised.

Cream together the cream cheese, icing sugar, egg, sifted custard powder, stir in the raisins, milk and oil and pour into the pastry case. Sprinkle with the chopped almonds or other nuts. Bake approx 35–40 minutes.

Milena's tip
All nuts may be successfully chopped in a food processor.

Chocolate and Walnut Cake

75 g (3oz) dark chocolate
2 tbsp of water
125 g (5 oz) icing sugar
125 g (5 oz) unsalted butter
3 eggs, separated
125 g (5 oz) walnuts, or
hazelnuts, roughly chopped
50 g (2 oz) plain flour
15 g ($^{1}/_{2}$ oz) yeast dissolved
in 1 tbsp warm water
Pinch of salt

Melt chocolate in two tablespoons of water over low heat (or in microwave) and cool. Cream together sugar and butter, add yolks, chopped nuts, chocolate and plain flour. Finally fold in stiffly beaten egg whites, pinch of salt and yeast dissolved in one tablespoon of warm water. Pour mixture into buttered and floured 20 cm (8 in) spring clip cake tin; stand in the Remoska lined with Magic Non-stick Liner to prevent tin scratching the base and bake for approx 35 minutes. Allow to cool, transfer onto a platter and dust with icing sugar. May also be decorated with whipped cream.

Courgette Slices with Lemon Glaze

125 g (5 oz) grated courgette
100 g (4 oz) icing sugar
2 tsp vanilla sugar
2 tbsp of vegetable oil
125 g (5 oz) self-raising
flour
50 g (2 oz) semolina
Handful of very finely
chopped walnuts

Lemon glaze
100 g (4 oz) icing sugar
1 egg white
Juice of $^{1}/_{2}$ lemon

Peel and grate courgette and mix with other ingredients. Knead the mix with wet hands, and with the aid of a spatula spread over base of the Remoska lined with baking parchment or 'Magic Non-stick Liner'. Cover with lid and bake until golden, approx 20–30 minutes. Cake (not very deep) is ready when cocktail stick inserted in the centre comes out clean.

Meanwhile, prepare lemon glaze. In a mixing bowl combine sugar, egg white, juice from half a lemon and whisk until thick smooth sauce forms. Spread over warm dessert and slice when cool.

Offer a prize to anyone guessing the ingredients!

Cream Cheese Bread and Butter Pudding

8 large slices of white bread
75 g (3 oz) unsalted butter
500 g (1 lb) soft cream-
cheese, Quark or Ricotta
3 eggs
50 g (2 oz) raisins soaked
for 15 minutes in dark rum
100 g (4 oz) caster sugar
Finely grated rind from
1 lemon
500 ml (1 pt) milk

Cut bread slices diagonally across into triangles, brush both sides with melted butter and place half in the base of the buttered Remoska. Mix cream cheese with two eggs, raisins, half of the sugar and grated lemon rind. Spread this mixture over the bread; cover with the rest of the buttered bread. Whisk up the third egg with the milk and pour over the prepared pudding, leaving it to soak for ten minutes before baking. Drizzle with any leftover melted butter, cover with lid and bake to golden crispy brown approx 30–40 minutes. Sprinkle with the rest of the sugar whilst still warm.

Melting Chocolate Dessert

125 g (5 oz) unsalted butter
125 g (5 oz) 70% plain
chocolate
2 eggs plus 2 egg yolks
4 tbsp caster sugar
2 tbsp sieved plain flour
6 x 8 cm (3 in) ramekin
dishes or foil containers

Melt the chocolate over hot water or microwave and stir in the butter. Whisk eggs, yolks and sugar until light and fluffy. Fold in the melted chocolate/butter and the sieved flour. Ladle into the lightly buttered and floured ramekins, place in the Remoska and bake for approx 12–14 minutes until a firm crust forms but (hopefully) still runny inside. Leave standing for a few seconds, then turn out upside down and serve with a lemon sorbet or vanilla ice cream.

This dessert may be prepared days ahead and stored in the fridge before cooking. It may also be frozen but must be left to defrost before baking.

Orange Cake

6 eggs, separated
175 g (6 oz) caster sugar
1 large orange
100 g (4 oz) plain flour
1 tsp sifted baking powder
50 g (2 oz) fine semolina
100 g (4 oz) ground walnuts
Pinch of salt
Orange slices for garnish
Whipped cream

Cream together yolks and sugar until fluffy. Grate the rind from well-scrubbed orange, peel and carefully remove the segments, cut up finely and together with the rind stir into the yolk and sugar mixture. Gradually stir in the sifted flour and baking powder alternately with semolina, stiffly beaten egg whites, ground walnuts and pinch of salt. Line Remoska with baking parchment or the Magic Non-Stick Liner or Cake Tin Liner and spoon in the cake mix. Cover and bake approx 45 minutes. Test using a cocktail stick in the middle to ensure the cake is ready.

Garnish cooled cake with whipped cream and orange slices.

Semolina Soufflé with Cherries

4 eggs, separated
1 grated rind of lemon
1 tbsp lemon juice
100 g (4 oz) icing sugar
50 g (2 oz) hazelnuts
100 g (4 oz) semolina
225 g (8 oz) cherries or other small fruit
2 tsp vanilla sugar
Unsalted butter and fine breadcrumbs for Remoska

In a bowl cream the egg yolks, grated lemon rind, one tablespoon of lemon juice and sugar. Fold in stiffly beaten egg whites, grated hazelnuts and semolina. Fold in the rinsed, pitted fruit tossed with vanilla sugar. Pour batter into buttered and breadcrumbed Remoska and bake until golden, approx 20–30 minutes.

Slice baked and cooled soufflé and sprinkle with vanilla sugar.

Milena's tip
The breadcrumbs help the soufflé to 'cling' to the side of the pan, a good tip when making any soufflé.

Shortcake – Probably the best in the world!

350 g (12 oz) plain flour
225 g (8 oz) unsalted butter, chilled
100 g (4 oz) caster sugar
Glacé cherries

Rub butter into flour and sugar to make pastry. A food processor is excellent for this, it is a rich mixture to handle. Divide pastry into four equal parts and roll each out into a circle 1 cm ($\frac{1}{2}$ in) thick. Pinch the edges between finger and thumb, mark out into four triangles and prick all over with a fork. Place a glacé cherry on each portion. Place in the Remoska and bake until light golden brown, approx 20 minutes.

Sumptuous Apple and Orange Pie

Filling
1 kg (2$\frac{1}{2}$ lb) Bramley apples
2 medium oranges
75 g (3 oz) caster sugar

Pastry
500 g (1 lb) plain flour
225 g (8 oz) unsalted butter
or pastry margarine
40 g (1$\frac{1}{2}$ oz) caster sugar
1 large egg
This will make
3x18 cm (7 in) pies

Peel and slice apples, grate orange rind and squeeze juice. Mix apples, orange rind and juice. Cook in Remoska until apples 'fall' then add sugar, turn out into a bowl and cool. Rub plain flour, butter or margarine and caster sugar to form crumbs. Add egg and mix to make pastry or use a food processor. Chill for 30 minutes.

Divide pastry into 6 equal portions. Roll out to 3 mm ($\frac{1}{8}$ in) thickness and place on 18 cm (7 in) ovenproof pie plate. Fill with a third of the apple/orange mixture. Wet the edges, top with similar rolled out pastry, cut round the edges and crimp. Brush with water and sprinkle with caster sugar. Place pie in the Remoska, bake for approx 20 minutes or until top is golden brown. Repeat twice.

Sweet Baked Bananas with Coconut

4 firm bananas
Unsalted butter for
coating Remoska
250 ml (8 fl oz) water
Juice of 1 lemon
2 heaped tbsp granulated
(or brown) sugar
Pinch of salt
4 heaped tbsp grated
coconut

Pour boiling water over unpeeled bananas and wait for peel to turn brown. This stops the bananas from turning black during baking. Peel, cut in half lengthwise and bake in the buttered Remoska approx 10–15 minutes. Remove and place on platter. Meanwhile, in a saucepan boil 250 ml (8 fl oz) water with lemon juice, sugar and a pinch of salt for five minutes. Pour this sauce over bananas and leave to cool. Sprinkle cooled bananas with coconut and serve.

Walnut Cake

225 g (8 oz) caster sugar
6 eggs, separated
100 g (4 oz) semolina
100 g (4 oz) ground walnuts
Pinch of salt

Chocolate Sauce
225 g (8 oz) dark chocolate
25 g (1 oz) softened unsalted
butter

Whisk sugar with six yolks until fluffy. Whisk egg whites until stiff. Alternately add to the sugar/yolk mixture the semolina, stiffly beaten egg whites, ground walnuts and a pinch of salt. Line Remoska with baking parchment or Magic Non-Stick Liner or a cake tin liner. Fill with the mixture and bake approx 45 minutes. Test using a cocktail stick in the middle to ensure the cake is ready. Finished cake may be cut in half and spread with cream filling or jam. Cover with chocolate sauce on top and sides and decorate with whipped cream. If you find the top of the cake is browning too quickly, cover with circle of Magic Non-stick Liner.

Milenas tip
Use a cocktail stick to test
a cake is properly cooked by
inserting it into the middle
of the cake, if it is ready it
should come out dry

Chocolate Sauce – Place broken up chocolate in small pan and melt slowly over low heat. Stir in butter and mix well to obtain a runny sauce. Pour onto the cake. Lightly tip the cake from side to side and you should get a very smooth surface. Allow the sauce to flow down the sides and smooth it around with a palette knife.

Wholemeal Walnut Bread

500 g (1 lb) strong
wholemeal flour

1 tsp salt

1 tsp sugar

1 1/2 tbsp oil

7 g sachet fast action
dried yeast

1 tbsp black treacle

275 ml (10 fl oz) warm water

50 g (2 oz) chopped walnuts

In a large bowl sift flour, salt and sugar together. Add the oil. Mix in the yeast, add the treacle and water. Mix to a loose dough and knead for 5 minutes. Finally mix in the walnuts. Mould into two cobs and place in the Remoska. Cover with a tea towel and stand in a warm place.

When doubled in size place lid on and bake for approx 30 minutes. Turn over and bake for five minutes more. Cool on a wire rack.

Yoghurt fruit cake

1 egg

100 g (4 oz) icing sugar

100 g (4 oz) self-raising flour

50 g (2 oz) semolina

125 g (5 oz) plain white
runny yoghurt, not the
'Greek' type

Pinch of salt

500 g (1 lb) fruit in season,
currants, cherries, plums,
strawberries, raspberries etc

Plain flour for fruit
Unsalted butter and plain
flour for Remoska

Cream egg with sugar, stir in sifted self-raising flour, semolina, yoghurt and a pinch of salt. Pour this mix into buttered and floured Remoska, cover and bake briefly until batter begins to set, (take a look after five minutes) take off the lid, placing it upside down away from you but don't switch it off. Dot with fruit lightly dusted with plain flour, replace lid and bake for approx 30 minutes or until the cake is golden brown.

Sauces and Flavoured Butters

Sauces cannot be cooked in the Remoska.
Nevertheless, they are part of several of the recipes
in this book to be used with a number of the meat,
fish and vegetable dishes.

Contents in this section

Anchovy Butter

50 g (2 oz) unsalted butter
2 tbsp anchovy paste
Pinch of sweet paprika

Cream the butter together with the anchovy paste and sweet paprika. Spread on toast or on fish dishes.

Béchamel sauce

500 ml (1 pt) milk, hot
One small onion stuck
with three cloves
One bay leaf
Two sprigs of thyme
Sprig of rosemary
3–4 peppercorns
2–3 parsley stalks
75 g (3 oz) unsalted butter
75 g (3 oz) plain flour
Salt and white pepper
Double cream–optional
but good!

For a good gratin you need a good Béchamel sauce. This is said to have been invented in France by Marquis de Béchamel, in the service of Louis XIV of France and here is his recipe.

Infuse the onion, bay leaf, thyme, rosemary, peppercorns and parsley stalks in the hot milk, leave for ten minutes and strain the milk. Leave to cool.

In a saucepan melt the butter over low heat, put all the sieved flour in the pan at one go and stir well with a wooden spoon until the mixture turns into a fine crumb texture. Gradually add the milk and stirring, bring to the boil. Adjust the seasoning and simmer for a further 12 minutes to thicken. Now, if you wish, add two tablespoons of double cream. You may, of course make the sauce just from the butter, flour, milk and the seasoning following the same method.

Cheese sauce

Make a Béchamel sauce and for 500 ml (1 pt) quantity add 100 g (4 oz) grated cheese while still warm. Stir to dissolve the cheese.

Garlic Butter

2 large garlic cloves
¹/2 tsp sweet paprika
50 g (2 oz) unsalted butter
Few drops of Worcestershire sauce
Salt and freshly ground black pepper

Stir crushed garlic and paprika into softened butter, drizzle with Worcestershire sauce and season. Form into a 'sausage' roll with hands dipped in cold water, wrap in aluminium foil and refrigerate. Cut off individual slices as needed.

Herb Butter

4 tbsp chopped parsley
50 g (2 oz) butter
A squeeze of lemon juice
Pinch of salt

Stir parsley into creamed butter, flavour with lemon juice, pinch of salt and form into a roll with hands dipped in cold water. Wrap in foil and store in the refrigerator. Slice into rounds as needed and place on prepared food immediately before serving. Herb butter is also delicious on toast.

Variation – Instead of parsley, use any other variety of fresh herb.

Mushroom Sauce

2 garlic cloves
1 onion
2 tbsp olive oil
225 g (8 oz) fresh mushrooms
500 g (1 lb) tomatoes
¹/2 tsp dried marjoram
Salt and freshly ground black pepper
175 ml (6 fl oz) mushroom stock (cube)
Handful of fresh parsley

Fry crushed garlic and onion in oil until translucent, add cleaned, sliced mushrooms and fry until they release juice. Stir in scalded, peeled, chopped tomatoes, add marjoram, season and continue to cook a further five minutes. Add stock and barely simmer a further ten minutes. Liquidise; add freshly chopped parsley.

Serve sauce either with meat or poultry, pasta or cooked rice.

Mustard Butter

*2 heaped tbsp mustard,
French or German,
according to preference*
50 g (2 oz) unsalted butter
1 small onion
*Salt and freshly ground
black pepper*

Stir mustard into softened butter, add extremely finely chopped onion, season lightly and form into a 'sausage' roll. Wrap in aluminium foil and refrigerate as in previous recipe. Cut off individual slices as needed. Use on toast, canapés, sandwiches, steak, and spread on chicken when roasting.

Mustard Sauce

100 g (4 oz) butter
*6 tbsp French or German
mustard*
150 ml (5 fl oz) double cream
1 tbsp plain flour
4 tbsp chopped parsley
1/2 tsp sweet paprika

Melt butter in pan on low heat and add mustard, stirring constantly. Don't boil, just heat through. Stir in cream mixed with plain flour, parsley, sweet paprika and heat just enough to cook the flour until the sauce thickens.

This sauce goes well with meat or fish.

Parsley Vinaigrette

2 large handfuls of parsley
4 anchovies
*Slice of rye bread with
crust cut off*
2 garlic cloves
Juice of 2 lemons
Few tbsp red wine vinegar
100 ml (4 fl oz) olive oil
1 heaped tbsp capers

Finely chop parsley, anchovies, crumble the bread and crush the garlic, mix together, add lemon juice and wine vinegar to taste. Whisk thoroughly. Put mixture in glass bowl or jar, add capers (if using) and olive oil. Leave to stand for two days in the refrigerator before using. The mixture must be constantly submerged in oil and stored in refrigerator to keep from spoiling. Shake before using. Use sauce like ketchup with meats, fish, or poured over hard-boiled eggs.

Pepper Sauce

1 large onion
2 tbsp olive oil
2 large peppers
500 g (1 lb) tomatoes
50 ml (2 fl oz) red wine vinegar
Salt and freshly ground black pepper
4 tbsp chopped parsley

Fry finely chopped onion in oil until translucent, add finely chopped peppers and continue frying. Stir in scalded, peeled, chopped tomatoes, add the vinegar (amount depends on type of vinegar, because sauce should not be too sour), season with salt and black pepper and simmer slowly until thickened. Finally stir in parsley. Pour cooled sauce into a jar and store in refrigerator. Shake before using. Serve with meat or fish, poultry or poured over hard-boiled eggs or cold cooked leeks.

Tomato Sauce

2 garlic cloves
2 tbsp olive oil
500 g (1 lb) ripe tomatoes
2 tsp caster sugar
Pinch of dried oregano or marjoram
Salt and freshly ground black pepper
Handful of fresh parsley

Fry crushed garlic in oil, add scalded, peeled, chopped tomatoes, sugar, oregano, season and cook until tomatoes are tender. Liquidise; finally stir in chopped parsley.

There are, of course, a great variety of very good tomato sauces on the shop shelves.

Walnut Butter

50 g (2 oz) soft butter
4 tbsp of ground walnuts
Salt

Cream the butter and work in the ground walnuts. Spread on toast, grilled meats or vegetables.

Vive la France

*I spent two years in France with a family as a governess
to two small boys. Marie was the family cook and I still
have some of the recipes she wrote down for me. Reading them I
realised how well some would adapt to the Remoska, so here
is a small selection.*

Contents in this section

Vive La France

Reading through my battered original edition of Elizabeth David's 'French Provincial Cooking' about her time spent with a family in Paris, I was reminded that before I married, in the early fifties, I spent two years in France with a family as a governess to two small boys. Marie was the family cook and I still have some of the recipes she wrote down for me. Reading them I realised how well some would adapt to the Remoska, so here is a small selection.

The Béchamel sauce mentioned throughout the book figures largely. Gratins were family favourites and food with the addition of the occasional spoonful of wine or brandy was not restricted to grownups. Marie's philosophy concerning gratins was, that it was an excellent way of using up leftovers, indeed, the expression – d'accomoder les restes – is often a chapter in many a French cookery book. It was also a subtle way of getting the boys to eat pasta, vegetables and anything else as long as it was covered with one of Marie's sauces.

The quantity is for four–six people, ideally in the 'Grand' Remoska, using an ovenproof dish that will fit comfortably in the Remoska pan. Line your Remoska with the Magic Non-stick Liner. Alternatively, cook the recipes directly in the Standard pan perhaps reducing the quantities by a quarter.

Milena Grenfell-Baines

Baked Peaches

6 slices of brioche bread
25 g (1 oz) unsalted butter
3 large ripe peaches
50 g (2 oz) crème fraiche
Caster sugar to taste

Butter each slice of brioche and place in a buttered Remoska pan–shallow is better. Peel the peaches by plunging them in boiling water for half a minute, the skins should slide off. Halve them and take out the stones. Sit each half on a slice of the brioche and sprinkle with a teaspoon of sugar. Cover and bake for approx ten minutes until the brioche is crisp and golden. Serve with the crème fraiche whipped with sugar to taste.

During the week fresh fruit and cheese were eaten at the end of the meal. 'Le Dessert' was a Sunday treat usually bought by 'Monsieur' in the 'best' patisserie.

Baked Stuffed Onions

6 large onions
300 g (10 oz) sausage meat from your favourite sausage
3 tbsp finely chopped parsley
3 garlic cloves, crushed
75 g (3 oz) Parmesan, grated
3 eggs, separated
2 tbsp flour
Salt and freshly ground black pepper
2 tsp curry powder
3 tbsp brandy
Butter
Dried breadcrumbs

Wash and carefully peel the onions so that you have a nice smooth surface. Cut off the top and carefully remove the centre so that you have at least one centimetre of a hollowed out 'wall'. Chop up the centres of the onions and mix with the sausage meat, parsley, the garlic cloves, the Parmesan (keeping back two heaped table-spoonfuls) and the three egg yolks. Mix it really well and fill the onion cavities leaving a little space at the top.

Whisk the whites until stiff, carefully fold in the flour, one tablespoon of Parmesan, curry powder, season and fill the space left in the onions. Sprinkle each onion with half a tablespoon of the brandy. Brush each onion with melted butter and make a nest from a piece of aluminium (it used to be crumpled baking paper), sit the onion in the nest and place in the Remoska. Sprinkle with the last of the Parmesan, the brandy and breadcrumbs, close the lid and bake for 30- 40 minutes.

Gnocchi à la Romaine – *Semolina squares with grated Parmesan*

300 g (10 oz) semolina
75 g (3 oz) butter
3 eggs
Salt and freshly ground black pepper
750 ml (1 1/2 pt) milk
50 g (2 oz) Parmesan, grated

Heat the milk in a pan and when it comes to the boil add the semolina, season with salt and a little pepper and with a wooden spoon stir well and simmer for ten minutes. Give it an occasional stir, it will become quite thick. Remove from the heat, cool a little and add the three eggs, making sure they are well mixed in. Pour onto a dampened pastry board (today you could use a sheet of the Magic Non-stick Liner) and smooth the mixture to one centimetre thickness with a damp palette knife. Leave to go cold and cut into 4 cm squares.

Generously butter your gratin dish or the Remoska pan, cover the base with a layer of the semolina squares, sprinkle with Parmesan, cover with another layer of semolina squares arranging them like roof tiles, sprinkle more Parmesan and dot with the rest of the butter.

Cover with the lid and cook until the Gnocchi take on a golden colour, approx 15 minutes– keep an eye on them.

Gratin of Chicory and Ham

900 g (2 lb) chicory
1 onion, finely chopped
Oil
8 fine slices of boiled ham
3 tbsp fresh breadcrumbs
1 teacup of milk
Salt and freshly ground
black pepper
50 g (2 oz) Gruyère, grated
250 ml (8 fl oz) Béchamel
sauce (see page 137)
Butter
Oil

Mostly used in the UK chopped up in a salad, chicory or 'endive' is delicious just braised in butter. The following is a tasty dish often served in France as a simple main course with a tomato side salad.

Wash the chicory well, boil in salted water, approx ten minutes and leave it to drain in a colander. Place it in a buttered gratin dish or the Remoska pan. Heat a little oil in a frying pan and fry the finely chopped onion to a golden colour. Mince the ham slices, soak the breadcrumbs in the milk and squeeze them out, stir the ham and the breadcrumbs with the onion and season with salt and pepper. Spread this mixture over the chicory, sprinkle half the cheese on, pour over the Béchamel sauce, cover with the rest of the cheese, close the lid or place your gratin dish in the Remoska and close the lid and bake for approx 10 – 15 minutes.

Gratin of Mussels with Garlic Butter

900 g (2 lb) of 'best' mussels
2 onions
Salt and freshly ground black pepper
4 garlic cloves, crushed
3 tbsp dried breadcrumbs
Large handful of parsley, very finely chopped
100 g (4 oz) unsalted butter
Olive oil
4 tbsp crème fraiche

Thoroughly wash the mussels under a tap of cold running water. Place them into a large pan of water into which you have cut up the two onions, bring to boil and simmer until the mussels open. Tip them into a colander, discard the onions, take the mussels out of their shells, rinse in tepid water and set the mussels aside.

Mix the crushed garlic with half the chopped parsley, season and work into softened butter to obtain a creamy spread. Generously oil the Remoska pan or a gratin dish and one by one put mounds of the creamy mixture on each mussel and place it in the Remoska or dish. Sprinkle with the rest of the parsley and the breadcrumbs. Drizzle with the crème fraiche and dot with butter. Bake for approx 15 minutes.

Gratin Savoyarde

500 ml (1 pt) full cream milk
1 tbsp oil
1 garlic clove
900 g (2 lb) waxy potatoes
Salt and freshly ground black pepper
Grating of nutmeg
Butter for gratin dish or Remoska
150 g (5 oz) Gruyère or Cheddar, grated
3 tbsp double cream

Pour milk into a large pan, add the oil, the whole garlic clove and slowly bring to boil. Peel and wash the potatoes. Finely slice them but do not wash again. Place in the simmering milk and cook until tender. Season and add a grating of nutmeg.

Butter a shallow gratin dish or the shallow Remoska pan (the deep one will serve but will take longer). Remove the potatoes with a slotted spoon and place in the chosen dish. Sprinkle with grated cheese and drizzle the cream over the cheese. Bake until cheese has melted and taken on a golden sheen approx 10–15 minutes.

La Galette – Walnut Pasty

Speciality of Sarlat in the Dordogne

Sweet short crust pastry
225 g (8 oz) plain flour
Pinch of salt
125 g (5 oz) butter
50 g (2 oz) caster sugar
1 egg yolk
1 or 2 tbsp of water
A loose based flan tin,
20 cm (9 in) diameter

For the filling
125 g (5 oz) shelled walnuts
2 level tbsp honey
150 ml (5 fl oz) single cream
A dusting of caster sugar

This is a very rich pastry best made in a food processor or sift the flour with a pinch of salt into a mixing bowl and using your fingertips very lightly rub in the butter. Add the caster sugar, then mix the pastry to a firm dough with the egg yolk and water.

Form half the pastry into an even round. Flatten the top then roll it out to the size of the base of the tin. Carefully roll it out fractionally larger than the base so that it will fit neatly to the top of the filling. Make three parallel cuts in the surface. Roll out the rest of the pastry 2 cm (1 in) larger than the base of the tin, lift it over a rolling pin into the tin and line the base, carefully pressing the pastry halfway up the sides of the tin. This pastry is quite fragile!

For the filling, roughly chop the nuts and mix them in a bowl with the honey. Keep aside a tablespoon of cream and stir the rest into the nuts and honey. Pour the mixture into the pastry and spread the nuts evenly over the surface. Carefully lift the pastry 'lid' into position and press the two edges of pastry round the inside edge with prongs of a fork. Brush the surface with the rest of the cream and sprinkle with caster sugar.

Place in the Remoska pan and bake approx 25 minutes until pastry is a golden colour. Leave to cool a little, then take out of the flan tin and cool completely.

Lamb in Wine sauce

1 1/2 kg (3 lb) breast of lamb
2 large carrots, sliced
2 large onions, sliced
1 large garlic clove, crushed
75 g (3 oz) flour seasoned
with salt and freshly ground
black pepper
1 tbsp Herbs of Provence
3 tbsp tomato concentrate
1 heaped tsp caster sugar
250 ml (8 fl oz) dry
white wine
500 ml (1 pt) water
Olive oil for frying

Cut the meat into serving pieces, trimming off all the fat. Put the flour in a plastic bag, (paper bag in those days), drop the meat in and shake it up to coat the meat. Don't throw away the flour. In a large frying pan brown the pieces of lamb really well on all sides in the olive oil, remove to the Remoska, add the carrots, onions and garlic to the pan and brown really dark – this helps to give the sauce a good colour.

Add the vegetables to the meat, add the herbs, the tomato concentrate and the flour left in the plastic bag. Stir until meat is well coated, use your judgment if you think more tomato concentrate is necessary. Add sugar, wine and water. Stir, cover and start cooking The sauce should thicken and reduce.

Half way (after 20 minutes) test the meat for tenderness and remove two ladlesful of the gravy. Place this in a pan and add enough water to cover the potatoes you have been peeling to eat with this dish. Ideally they should be new potatoes. With the help of the added gravy they should have a lovely rosy colour when boiled.

Check on the lamb. It should be tender after a total of 40 minutes cooking.

Onion Tart

Pastry to line a 20cm (8 in) loose bottomed flan tin or the shallow pan of the standard Remoska

Enough sliced raw onions to fill the pan well packed twice over. This will cook down to the correct amount.

Vegetable oil
3 eggs
1 tbsp caster sugar
Salt and freshly ground black pepper
200 g (7 oz) Gruyère or Cheddar, grated
2 tbsp double cream or crème fraiche

Cover the base of a largish pan with oil to a depth of about 2 cm, add the onion and sugar. Cook very slowly, do not fry, until the onions take on a pale golden colour. Drain off all the oil. Place the onions in a bowl, stir in the whisked eggs, two thirds of the cheese and the cream. Pour the cooled mixture into the pastry lined chosen tin, sprinkle the rest of the cheese on top and bake until the pastry is cooked and the filling firm to touch, approx 30 minutes.

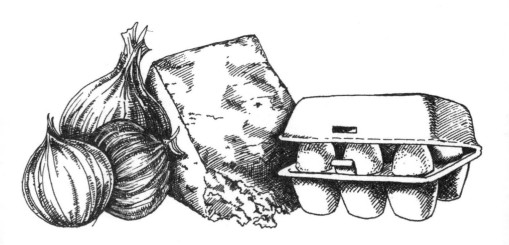

Rabbit with Prunes, Olives and Bacon

For the marinade
275 ml (10 fl oz) red wine
2 tbsp olive oil
1 large onion, coarsely chopped
1 large carrot, coarsely chopped
10 peppercorns
Bay leaf

1 large dressed rabbit, cut into pieces
100 g (4 oz) prunes, stoned
2 tbsp oil
1 tbsp plain flour
275 ml (10 fl oz) red wine
275 ml (10 fl oz) chicken stock
2 garlic cloves, finely chopped
Bouquet garni
150 g (5 oz) streaky bacon, rinded and cut into strips
75 g (3 oz) black olives, stoned and halved
Salt and freshly ground black pepper

Mix the marinade ingredients in a bowl and add the rabbit and prunes. Stir well and leave in a cool place for 2–3 hours or overnight, stirring occasionally.

Using a slotted spoon remove the rabbit, prunes and vegetables from the marinade and pat dry. Heat the oil in a large frying pan and brown the rabbit pieces in it. Remove the rabbit, place in the Remoska pan and in the frying pan brown the vegetables, sprinkle in the flour and sauté for a minute or so. Stir in the marinade, wine, and stock together with the garlic, bouquet garni and seasoning and bring to a boil. Pour all the contents of the frying pan over the rabbit in the Remoska, close the lid and cook for approx 30 minutes.

Towards the end of this time dry fry the bacon until crisp. Add this, the olives and prunes to the Remoska and cook for a further 15 minutes. Transfer the rabbit and the olives, prunes etc to a serving dish. Pour the remaining juices into a saucepan; boil rapidly to reduce to a sauce.

Milena's tip
Bouquet garni–two or three stalks of parsley, a sprig of thyme and a bay leaf tied in a piece of muslin.

Seafood Pancakes

Best in shallow pan

*6 pancakes or you may
use 225 g (8 oz) cannelloni
cooked and follow same recipe*

*60 g (2½ oz) butter
40 g (1½ oz) flour
175 ml (6 fl oz) milk
3 tbsp crème fraiche
225 g (8 oz) crab meat or
large prawns–langoustines
125 g (5 oz) button
mushrooms
1 tbsp brandy
Freshly ground white pepper
1 yolk of egg
Grating of nutmeg
150 g (5 oz) Gruyère, grated*

Having made your pancakes or boiled and drained the cannelloni – make your filling in the following manner – but first prepare your Béchamel, see page 137, with the butter, flour and milk and add the crème fraiche. Finely cut up your chosen seafood, stir in a bowl with half the Béchamel, very finely chopped mushrooms, the tablespoon of brandy, check for seasoning and simmer for a 'little' (her word) five minutes. Stir in 100 g (4 oz) of the grated cheese.

Place a good tablespoon of the filling on each pancake or the cannelloni, roll up and place in the buttered Remoska. Cover all with the rest of the Béchamel into which you first stir the egg yolk, season with pepper and nutmeg. Sprinkle with the rest of the Gruyère, put the lid on and bake for approx 15 minutes.

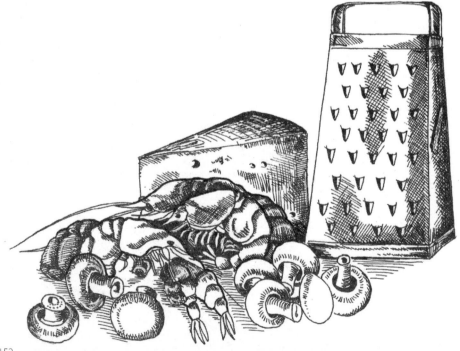

Spinach Tagliatelli Gratin with Créme Fraiche Sauce

*300 g (10 oz) tagliatelli
spinach pasta*

*Simple Béchamel
75 g (3 oz) butter
50 g (2 oz) plain flour
500 ml (1 pt) milk*

*150 g (5 oz) button
mushrooms
200 g (7 oz) boiled ham
Butter for greasing dish
or Remoska*

*Breadcrumbs
2 eggs
Salt and freshly ground
black pepper
50 g (2 oz) Parmesan, grated
500 ml (1 pt) crème fraiche
2 tsp curry powder
1 small black truffle!*

Cook the pasta for five minutes, drain and rinse with cold water. Prepare a 'butter rich' Béchamel with the butter, flour and milk and while it is still warm, stir in roughly chopped mushrooms and the ham cut in short fine batons. Gently stir all this into the tagliatelli.

Butter an ovenproof dish or the Remoska, sprinkle base and sides with the breadcrumbs and pour in the pasta mix. Whisk up the eggs, season, add the Parmesan and pour over the pasta. Cover and cook until you have a lovely crunchy crust, approx 20 minutes.

Whisk the crème fraiche with the curry powder, finely grate the small black truffle and incorporate into the curried cream. The gratin should be served hot with the sauce passed round to help oneself.

Notes

Notes

Notes

Notes

Notes